DRAMA AND RITUAL OF EARLY HINDUISM

PERFORMING ARTS SERIES

General Editor

FARLEY P. RICHMOND

VOLUME IV

Drama and Ritual of Early Hinduism

Natalia Lidova

Foreword by
Kapila Vatsyayan

MOTILAL BANARSIDASS PUBLISHERS
PRIVATE LIMITED • DELHI

First Edition: Delhi, 1994

ISBN: 81-208-1234-9

Also available at:

MOTILAL BANARSIDASS

41 U.A. Bungalow Road, Jawahar Nagar, Delhi 110 007
120 Royapettah High Road, Mylapore, Madras 600 004
16 St. Mark's Road, Bangalore 560 001
Ashok Rajpath, Patna 800 004
Chowk, Varanasi 221 001

PRINTED IN INDIA

BY JAINENDRA PRAKASH JAIN AT SHRI JAINENDRA PRESS,
A-45 NARAINA, PHASE I, NEW DELHI 110 028
AND PUBLISHED BY NARENDRA PRAKASH JAIN FOR
MOTILAL BANARSIDASS PUBLISHERS PVT. LTD.,
BUNGALOW ROAD, DELHI 110 007

FOREWORD BY SERIES EDITOR

India is one of the great repositories of performing arts, particularly those of the classical, folk/popular, devotional and modern traditions. The sheer enormity and diversity of its cultural expressions in music, dance, dance/drama and theatre are the envy of many nations around the world. This series intends to assemble some of the best books now available on these subjects.

Without exaggeration, a series such as this would not have been possible twenty years ago when I first began writing about Indian theatre. At that time little more than a few dozen books comprised the entire field of scholarship in the English language, not to mention the paucity of materials in regional Indian languages. Today that picture has radically changed. Numerous publishers have devoted precious press time to volumes of well-illustrated, detailed and, yes, sometimes even esoteric works on the multiple aspects of this fascinating subject. Comb any bookshop in Delhi or Madras, Bombay or Calcutta and you will regularly find new works appearing on the shelves. This represents a real area of growth! It is to the credit of Motilal Banarsidass that there is now the potential of assembling numerous volumes together under one umbrella.

Specialized studies such as Natalia Lidova's *Drama and Ritual of Early Hinduism* further our understanding of the depth and richness of the Indian performance tradition. This is particularly true when the study focuses on the roots of theatre in the distant past. This welcome book sets out to explore the foundations of theatre in ritual practice. In a careful, systematic way Lidova lays out a process by which the classical Sanskrit theatre may have come into existence. Scholars have wrestled with this question for centuries. Because of this work we have a better understanding of the process. The work is bound to encourage further speculation about this topic in the years to come.

FARLEY P. RICHMOND

FOREWORD

The *Nāṭyaśāstra* has attracted the attention of scholars, now for over a hundred years. The discovery of fragments of the manuscript was as important an event, as the discovery of the manuscript of *Abhijñana Śākuntalam* by William Jones. Elsewhere, I have traced the history of critical scholarship on the *Nāṭyaśāstra* from J. Grosset to Selyvin Levi, P.V. Kane, S.K. De, V. Raghavan, K.C. Pandey, Masson, F.B.J. Kuiper, S.C. Bhatt; M.Ch. Byrski and also Indushekhar. The text presents challenges to any serious student of the Indian culture, particularly the arts and specifically, the theatre arts. Historians of Indian literature, particularly, Sanskrit literature and theatre, have debated heatedly on the origins of the Indian theatre from divergent theoretical positions. While some have examined the text of the *Nāṭyaśāstra* by tacitly accepting the Greek influence on Indian culture, sculpture and the theatre, others have examined the text as a direct evolution of Vedic speculative thought and Brahmanical ritual. The spectrum of opinions range from the origins of theatre and the aesthetics of the *Nāṭyaśāstra* to its structure and technique. Divergent views have been expressed and the debate continues.

Parallel have been the attempts at editing the text of the *Nāṭyaśāstra* and the indispensable commentary of Abhinava Gupta, known as *Abhinavabhārati.* F.-E. Hall, W. Heymann, P. Regnaud, J. Grosset, Sivadatta and Parab, Kedarnath, Ramakrishna Kavi, Manmohan Ghosh and others have painstakingly attempted to edit in part or whole the authentic text of the *Nāṭyaśāstra* with or without its most important commentary: *Abhinavabhārati.*

To have the courage to re-investigate a text and its interpretation, with as long and complex a history, is in itself commendable. Further, to do this sitting in Moscow at a time when access to many materials may not have been easy, is equally brave.

Dr Natalia Lidova reopens the debate on the origin of Sanskrit theatre *de novo,* specially, the relationship between ritual and drama. She questions the hypothesis that the *Nāṭyaśāstra* reflects a direct evolution of theatre from Vedic ritual (*Yajña*). Instead, she makes the connection between *Yajña* and *Pūjā* and relates the textual evidence in the *Nāṭyaśāstra* with the rituals described in the

Śaiva Āgamas. The hypothesis of making a clear distinction between the Vedic *Yajña* and what she terms as "non-Vedic *Pūjā*" is basic to her argument. The problem of establishing a rough, if not an exact chronology of the Vedic *Yajña* and the *Śaiva Āgamas* as both being the precursors of the *Nāṭyaśāstra* or at least contemporary, is a field which, no doubt, will stimulate further questions and discussions. Dr Lidova makes a very interesting connection between what she terms as the Vedic tradition, its myths and even religious ideas, with those she connects with what she calls "non-Vedic *Pūjā* and Rituals". Textual and archaeological evidence, so far, has placed the emergence of a full and evolved methodology of *Pūjā* in the temples to a period later than the *Nāṭyaśāstra.* Dr Lidova's hypothesis would, undoubtedly, reopen the question of this chronology. Underlying her argument is the acceptance of the view that the *Nāṭyaśāstra* evolved over a period of many centuries. There is so far no complete consensus on whether the *Nāṭyaśāstra* is a cohesive text of a single author or is a composite compilation. Recent scholarship on the text points to unifying principles which run through the thirty-six chapters. Dr Lidova's interpretation will, undoubtedly, reopen the question of which section constitutes the "Kernel" and what are additions or interpolations.

Despite these tantalizing unresolved questions, the author has interpreted the text in a fascinating manner, specially the Chapter dealing with the *Pūrvaraṅga.* Equally engaging is her analysis of the different types of *nāṭaka* genres, specially the *Samavakāra, Dīma, Ihamṛga* as the stage versions of Vedic myths. The Chapter of her book dealing with *Ritual Drama in Early Hindu Culture* again re-investigates the relationship of *Yajña-pūjā,* a subject of continuing interest in many fields and on many levels. Dr Natalia Lidova examines closely the critical writing of her predecessors, particularly, Kuiper, in the context of *the Pūrvaraṅga.* She reconstructs the *Pūrvaraṅga* rites from the text and is fairly convincing. While there could, no doubt, be major differences of opinion with her interpretation of some of the technical terms, particularly *Citra,* she is more convincing in her singling out the supreme importance of the physical and conceptual notion of a centre. Rightly, she repeatedly draws attention to this. The centre, no doubt, corresponds to the place of Brahmā—the principle of totality—and from it emerge the *Brahmamaṇḍala* and

Brahmasthāna. Also, her identification of the *Jarjara*, with the principle of verticality, the *axis mundi* is well taken.

Also, there could be no difference of opinion with her view that the stage is, without doubt, a micro-replica of the Universe and the *Pūrvaraṅga* is the schematic statement in theatrical terms.

Dr Lidova, possibly, did not have access to some recent work on the *Nāṭyaśāstra* where the interconnection between Indian speculative thought, the techniques of Brahmānical ritual (*Yajña*) and the methodology of ritual have already been elaborated. Nevertheless, her analysis provides room for an alternate or complimentary line of inquiry.

The Chapter on *Drama as Stage Version of Myths* opens up many new avenues of the interpretation of the myths and their recreation or re-enactment on the stage. More important is her interpretation of different types of plays (*Nāṭaka)* and her making a one-to-one correspondence between the myth and the type of play.

Dr Lidova's Chapter on *The Ritual Drama in Early Hindu Culture* and the construction of the stage is yet another dimension of the *Nāṭyaśāstra* which remains a subject of discussion and debate. It eludes final resolution. Dr Lidova makes a connection between the *Nāṭyaśāstra* precepts of theatre construction, the architectural treatises and the Āgamic treatises. She suggests that the play-house (theatre) itself was a templar structure which was almost a precursor or was at least co-eval with actual temples. She identifies the seminal term *guhā*, cave to develop her argument. Further, she believes that perhaps the anthropomorphic forms of deities in Indian sculpture were conditioned by the symbolism of "actor's costumes, movements and make-up". In this connection she makes an important statement, viz. "evidently the *pūjā* could not acquire the first cult imagery before the stage gave final shape to the anthropomorphous likeness of the Hindu pantheon. The three kinds of divine incarnation—through the actor in the drama, through the priest performing the *pūjā* and through the sculptor as he worked with stone, wood or metal—share a symbolism and appeal to one system of ritual ideas." This conclusion provides scope for further investigation by not only the historians of Indian texts—Vedic and Āgamic—but also the archaeologists and historians of the theatre arts. So far *Yajña-pūjā* relationship has been viewed in a sequential order. Dr Lidova points out concurrent developments and interactions. Meticulously, she examines the etymology of the word *pūjā*, the Dravaḍian roots, and the implications of the incorporation of another stream into the *Nāṭyaśāstra*, thereby giving it the place of a templar structure. Although we cannot assume that there were temple structures before the writing of the *Nāṭyaśāstra* in the absence of archaeological evidence, Dr Lidova also gives some reasons for why these structures may not have been found archaeologically and it is hoped that one day these will be. Serious scholarship often emerges from deep insight and a scholar searches for and explores evidence for the insights. Dr Lidova's text is full of very sensitive insights into this text and I have no doubt that it will evoke further scholarship, both linguistic and archaeological, to support not only conceptually, but, historically the hypothesis on which she works. She herself provides some evidence.

I am delighted that we should get another fresh look at a perenially valid fountainhead of Indian drama. I would like to compliment Dr Lidova for this most serious, painstaking and diligent task of looking at a very difficult and problematic text. This is an important contribution to critical scholarship on the *Nāṭyaśāstra*. I look forward to the responses that it will evoke from the community of scholars, not only of the text, but, also Indian culture.

KAPILA VATSYAYAN

CONTENTS

LIST OF ABBREVIATIONS

AbhBh—Abhinavabhārati of Abhinavagupta
Aj—Ajitāgama
AitBr—Aitareya Brāhmaṇa
AnSū—Anupada Sūtra
AnŚrSū—Anupada Śrauta Sūtra
AśvŚrSū—Āśvalāyana Śrauta Sūtra
Ath—Atharvaveda
BhPr—Bhāvaprakāśa of Śāradātanaya
BṛUp—Bṛhadāraṇyaka Upaniṣad
ChUp—Chāndogya Upaniṣad
DR—Daśarūpa of Dhanañjaya
GopBr—Gopatha Brāhmaṇa
MaitSam—Maitrāyaṇī Saṃhitā
Mṛg—Mṛgendrāgama
NLRK—Nāṭakalakṣaṇaratnakośa of Sāgaranandin
ND—Nāṭyadarpaṇa
NŚ—Nāṭyaśāstra
Pāṇ—Pāṇini Aṣṭādhyāyī
Pat—Patañjali Mahābhāṣya
Raur—Rauravāgama
ṚV—Ṛgveda Saṃhitā
ŚBr—Śatapatha Brāhmaṇa
SD—Sāhityadarpaṇa
TaitSam—Taittiriya Saṃhitā
Vārt—Vārttikas of Kāṭyāyana

INTRODUCTION

The birth of art is a mystery. To raise its veil is one of the most formidable goals of humanities. The impact of the ritual on the emergence of the arts appears indisputable, but we can only rarely reconstrue the formal genesis from particular texts, rather than at the intuitive or generalized imaginative level. Ancient Indian texts give us this rare chance, with their detailed descriptions of rites and ample testimony on the archaic cultural tradition.

Among these manuscripts is the *Nāṭyaśāstra*, one of the oldest and, possibly, the most enigmatic texts Indian culture has to offer. The name of this treatise is made of two Sanskrit words: *Nāṭya*, theatre, scenic action or, more specifically, drama, and *Śāstra*, the term accepted in the Indian tradition for holy writ dedicated to a particular field of knowledge. As is often the case with ancient Indian texts, we can hardly say anything for sure about the *Nāṭyaśāstra*—either about the time it was written, or the author, or again, the mission meant for this grandiose cyclopaedia which stood at the cradle of the ancient Indian tradition of general artistic concept. Here, hypotheses are the lot of the contemporary scholar.

As students of this treatise repeatedly pointed out, it has no equal in the scope of information and thematic range among analogous ancient and medieval writings[1]. Really, its 36 chapters treat extremely diverse subjects: the ritual and mythology, as connected with the early mysterial performances; the characterization of the developed literary drama, which posed purely aesthetic, rather than sacral goals and proceeded from well-elaborated principles of acting; and last but not least, the theory of the drama, which includes a genre typology and an analysis of the formal structure of the Sanskrit drama. This thematic versatility reveals a multi-level content reflecting both archaic ideas of the ritual sources of the Indian theatre, close to the time of its birth, and later information from the era of the classical Sanskrit drama[2]. The legendary author of the *Nāṭyaśāstra*, the sage Bharata Muni, received his knowledge of dramatic art from none other than Brahmā. Nevertheless, as even the initial attempts to analyse the content of this treatise showed, it was not written from beginning to end as a single book, and lacked sufficient redaction. Most probably, it was the fruit of many authors' efforts, whose names have not gone down to us, and who, throughout centuries, developed and passed on the knowledge of the drama[3].

We do not know when the *Nāṭyaśāstra* emerged. All datings accepted in science come from oblique ratiocination. Contemporary Western Indology names the 1st and 2nd centuries A.D. as the most probable. However, even this dating points at a conventionalized period when the whole was compiled which the following centuries recognized as canonical. Doubtless, the compiler of the version that came down to us had a long tradition of drama theory to proceed from. Possibly, it was in the early centuries A.D. that he brought together the basic works on the theatre in a compendium of universal message.

Still, we can't limit the dating problem to the question when the extant version emerged. Its multi-level text and the dates based on cultural historical information provided by the treatise are separated by more than a millennium, from the 5th century B.C. to the 7th A.D.[4] As they seek to substantiate extreme views, scholars attempt to single out the oldest kernel of this book or, on the contrary, the latest stage of its formation, when the text already included all interpolations from different times. Strictly speaking, it has no precise date. No doubt, a major part appeared long before the 1st and 2nd centuries A.D., when, shortly before the classic Sanskrit drama reached its peak, the early text was brought into order and supplemented with information which corresponded to the actual stage practice of the time. As we see it, that time saw many archaic concepts reappraised to receive more topical interpretations. At the later developmental stages of the drama, the *Nāṭyaśāstra* was enriched with new interpolations corresponding to the latest achievements. The book not merely incorporates all these levels, coming from different times, but interlinks and blends them with each other. To distinguish between them is a challenge for the scholar. Without this indispensable, though often intuitive part of the work, we can't understand and correctly appreciate the developmental patterns of the Indian theatre[5]. As it is, the scholar who traces down the genesis of the drama proceeding from the *Nāṭyaśāstra* has to limit his effort to careful reconstruction whose laws are to a great extent determined by the treatise itself. In particular, when the canonical version was emerging, the drama was understood as a literary work made according to formal genre patterns, and the bulk of information about the birth of the theatre was already seen as legendary even by the authors of the treatise, and so was included in the *Nāṭyaśāstra* as the mythic tribute to an ancient and highly influential tradition. As we see it, however, the myths and legends on the genesis of the theatre, and detailed descriptions of scenic rites reflect the actual situation in which the theatre was born and, on the whole, provide a reliable historical picture of the ritual-drama correlation.

* * *

The origin of Sanskrit drama has interested scholars for a long time as crucial for our understanding of the many aspects of old Indian culture. Still, the goal is not attained to this day though the problem has been studied for over a century and numerous hypotheses have come up. The scholarly argument concentrates on two basic questions: (1) whether the Sanskrit drama had a ritual or secular background and (2) when and in what ethnic and cultural milieu it first emerged.

Depending on their answers to these questions, experts offer their hypotheses of the independent evolution of the Sanskrit drama or outlandish influences on it; they find its sources in the Aryan or non-Aryan Indian cultures, and trace it to the hoary antiquity or to a time close to the current era[6].

The theories we know as ritualistic are better substantiated and more consistent than those which connect the genesis of the drama with the folk theatrical tradition. At the same time, the ritualistic theories disagree on the crucial issue of ritualistic practices, which lie at the basis of the Indian theatre. They take it for granted that it is both necessary and sufficient for the proof of its sacral origin to find immediate links between the earlier dramatic forms and particular rites which, in the final analysis, indicate the time and milieu in which the drama appeared.

In most instances, the search for the ritual was connected with the Vedic ritualistic and mythological system. As scholars proceeded from the idea of drama-ritual structural closeness, they tried to find sacral sources of the drama in the dialogue hymns of the Ṛgveda. The hymnal form which demanded two or more participants implied that they could be enacted by several priests during offering ceremonies[7]. However, this interpretation of Ṛgvedic dialogues and the attempts to see them as scattered fragments of Vedic mystery widespread in the Indo-European antiquity met with well-substantiated criticisms which pointed out that neither the Ṛgveda nor later priestly texts (as *Brāhmaṇas* and *Śrauta Sūtras*) contained direct or oblique practical information about the existence of particular rites where dialogue hymns could be used. A.B.Keith saw it as sufficient reason to deny ritual and magical content to these dialogues, which he qualified as secular hymns[8]. As P. Time pointed out, the Ṛgvedic dialogues every time fixed a static situation and did not show action in its development, which is a *sine qua non* for the formation of the drama[9].

Apart from dialogue hymns, the *Somakrayaṇa* and *Mahāvrata* rites also attracted scholarly attention—both spectacular for their pageantry among other Vedic rites[10]. Hence the assumption that the theatrical elements formed in their depth served as starting-point for the ancient Indian drama.

An immediate link between these rituals and the drama was never traced, and these concepts stayed plausible hypotheses which however defied proof. It is difficult to deny that any well-developed ceremonial rite performed to large congregations contains scenic elements, and is not only sacral action but a mystery play of a kind. There is, however, ample historical proof that the mere presence of dramatic rites in a ritualistic culture does not in itself presuppose the emergence of the drama. Many ancient regions knew theatrical rites but these did not evolve into the drama.

Repeated attempts to see the sources of the theatre in the particular Vedic rites made even convinced partisans of the ritual origins of the ancient Indian drama follow their no less convinced opponents in acknowledging that "the Vedic hymns and the ritual were not the immediate precursors of the classical drama."[11]

* * *

F.B.J. Kuiper's theory belongs to the latest and well-argumented concepts of the ritualistic origin of the ancient Indian theatre, as put forward in his book, "Varuṇa and Vidūśaka: On the Origin of the Sanskrit Drama"[12]. The author turns to the *Nāṭyaśāstra*, unlike his predecessors, who sought for testimony to the emergence of the drama in Vedic texts. Kuiper discovered traces of the Vedic mentality in its ritualistic and mythological content, concluding that the first dramas were scenic representations of the Vedic cosmogony and re-created Indra's struggle with the Asuras.[13] He distinguished between the drama proper and the *Pūrvaraṅga*, which preluded every performance and in which he saw a singular ritual act of crucial religious importance on a par with the drama, as against its accepted concept as the prologue.

As he saw it, the *Nāṭyaśastra* rituals were equivalent to the *yajña*, Vedic sacrifice.[14] Making this conclusion, the scholar referred not to a particular rite of the *yajña* kind but to the Vedic ritualism as a whole. He ascribed the impossibility to precisely re-create the rite which stood at the cradle of the theatre to the fact that "since only a part of the top of the iceberg of Vedic culture is visible in the priestly literature, there is no reason to expect that the starting-point for the later evolution of the drama can be found here."[15] His task was not so much to single out a particular rite as to show the characteristics of the ritualistic mentality as determining the scenic ritual and the plots of the earliest dramas, so Kuiper elaborated an original method to study the genesis of the Sanskrit drama.

However fruitful this method might be, and however, plausible the proofs of his numerous observations, we can't but name at least two disputable points in his concept: as he regards the scenic ritual, Kuiper stresses, above all, what he can link to the Vedic world outlook; his treatment of the rites mentioned in the treatise as equivalents of the *yajña*, and overlooks the fact that the *Nāṭyaśāstra* itself does not apply the word to these rites, referring to them as *pūjā*.

Here, the name of the rite is of vital importance, since the Indian tradition mutually counterpoised *yajña* and *pūjā* to an extent. At any rate they were topical at different stages of its evolution. The *yajña* was central in the Vedic era as a ceremonial rite, while *pūjā* became widespread in the post-Vedic time to come to the foreground as the basic Hindu ritual[16]. The very character of the ceremonies accompanying both has striking distinctions, too: Vedism had bloody offerings on special altars, as against Hindu bloodless sacrifices of incense, flowers and water before the images of divinity. The sophisticated symbolism and magic of the *yajña* contrasted with the simplified aestheticism of the *pūjā*, as the personal message of the former, performed for a particular donor (*yajamāna*), contrasted with the public character of the latter—a rite dedicated to a god in the name of all worshippers.

The very absence of references to the link between scenic rituals and the *yajña*, and direct references to *pūjā* in the *Nāṭyaśāstra* make us put to doubt the interpretation of the rituals described in it as *yajña* equivalents, and again wonder which rite gave rise to the Sanskrit drama, and in which culture, Vedic or non-Vedic, we ought to seek its sources. These issues are the basic content of this book.

CHAPTER I

RITUAL TEXTS IN THE *NĀṬYAŚĀSTRA*

THE *PŪRVARAṄGA*

The *Nāṭyaśāstra* describes rituals in Chapters II, III and V, which characterize three basic rites connected with the ancient Indian scenic practice: the foundation and consecration of a theatre—both performed only once in the new building—and the *Pūrvaraṅga*, repeated before every performance.

This long ceremony had two parts. The first began on stage, with the curtain closed, while the second went on before the audience. Musical instruments were arranged and the musicians took their seats behind the curtain during the *Pratyāhāra*—the opening—which proceeded to the *Avataraṇa*, when the singers followed them, *Ārambha*, vocal exercises, and *Āśrāvaṇa*, the tuning of instruments. Then several performing manners were rehearsed (*Vaktrapāṇi*), the instrument players tightened their strings for the desired sound (*Parighaṭṭanā*), and did conventional manual gestures to indicate the rhythm (*Saṃghoṭanā*) till the sound of the strings merged with the drums (*Mārgāsārita*), the rhythm was verified (*Āsārita)* and, finally, started the *Gītavidhi* hymn in honour of the gods (*NŚ*.5.17-21).

At first sight, all these *Pūrvaraṅga* stages may seem purely technical, natural before a stage performance. However, the *Nāṭyaśāstra* qualifies them as sacral, not merely applied—unique forms of worship. Thus, *Pratyāhāra* serves Nāgas and *Rākṣasas, Apsaras* take pleasure in *Avataraṇa, Gandharvas* in *Ārambha, Dānavas* in *Āśrāvaṇa* and *Vaktrapāṇi*. Again, *Rākṣasa* hosts enjoy *Parighaṭṭanā,* Guhyakas *Saṃghoṭanā* and Yakṣas *Mārgāsārita,* while the hymn *Gītavidhi* sounds in honour of all gods (*NŚ*.5.45-50). Thus, this behind-the-curtain part of the *Pūrvaraṅga* is indispensable from the ritual viewpoint as tribute to *Rākṣasa* and *Dānava* demons, the lower deities—*Gandharvas, Apsaras, Guhyakas* and *Yakṣas*—and all gods[17].

The part performed before the audience included ten more obligatory episodes: a ritual song of the *Madraka* or *Vardhamānaka* type with an accompanying dance, *Utthāpana, Parivartana, Nāndī, Śuṣkāpakṛṣṭā, Raṅgadvāra, Cārī, Mahācārī, Trigata* and *Prarocana* (*NŚ*.5.12-15)—all these also of a symbolic ritual meaning, as worship of the principal Hindu gods. The *Vardhamānaka* song and dance extolled Rudra. *Utthāpana*—the start of the scenic part of the ceremony—signified the raising of the *jarjara*, Indra's banner and weapon which protected the *Nāṭya* from demons. *Parivartana* was served in honour of the *Lokapālas*—protectors of the world and the four cardinal point[18]. *Nāndī*, hymn to gods, Brahmins and the King, was said in honour of Soma. *Śuṣkāpakṛṣṭā* was a canticle to *jarjara* and the hosts of *Pitṛs*, ancestors. *Raṅgadvāra*, before the performance, with verbal and gesticular inclusions, worshipped Viṣṇu. *Cārī*—a combination of movements expressing joy (*Śṛṅgāra Rasa*)—worshipped Umā[19], while *Mahācārī*, a sequence of gesticular expressions of awe (*Raudra Rasa*) served Śiva. The conversation between *Sūtradhāra*, company leader, and his two assistants, *Pāripārśvaka*, was known as *Trigata*. The final part, *Prarocanā*, praised the drama, hinted at its plot and wished the performers success. According to the *Nāṭyaśāstra*, the *Pūrvaraṅga* as a whole "should be a *pūjā* to gods and is a *pūjā* to gods, conducive of *dharma*, fame and longevity, and pleasing the *Daityas*, and the *Dānavas*, as well as the denizens of the celestial world" (*NŚ*.5.57-58).

Most *Pūrvaraṅga* stages were accompanied by ritual songs (*Dhruvā*), with rhythm and tempo specified in Chapter V of the *Nāṭyaśāstra*. These detailed instructions as to the singing and instrumental accompaniment did not appear by chance. The entire *Pūrvaraṅga* is subjected to music, the kernel of the scenic action, the unseen director and conductor of the entire rite. At first slow, the tempo gradually quickened and became louder as the *Pūrvaraṅga* went on to reach its peak at the principal instant of the offering. The ritual events gained a suspense, proceeded to a climax and then denouement in correspondence to it.

A unique, celestial music accompanying the *Pūrvaraṅga* belonged to the *Gāndharva* system (*NŚ*.28.9). According to ancient Indian musicological treatises and the music sections of the *Nāṭyaśāstra*[20], this music could be played only with ritual ceremonies to give the congregation a proper mood and make it part of the performance, and thus played an essential sacral role.

Characteristically, depending on the rhythm and tempo, the treatise singles out two *Pūrvaraṅga* varieties, the *Caturasra* and the *Tryasra*. Each included all above-listed stages, the only and essential difference being that *Caturasra* had 16 bars, as against 12 in *Tryasra* (*NŚ*.5.87-88; 143-144). According to the *Nāṭyaśāstra* the measure not merely set the rhythm and tempo of song and instrumental music but determined the performers' movements (*NŚ*.5.149). Thus, *Parivarta,* steps round the stage, repeated throughout the rite, demanded sixteen movements and gestures in *Caturasra,* and twelve in *Tryasra,* with one step or gesture for one bar, quick or slow, depending on the music (*NŚ*.5.151). All this shows close dependence of performers' movements on the music. Every scenic movement, precisely determined and subjected to the rhythm, had a ritual meaning. The basis of the scenic movement, sequences of dancing steps, known as *Sūcī Cārī*[21], started now with the right foot, now with the left, allowing the performers to change position in the ritual space.

Both *Caturasra* and *Tryasra* included an *Utthāpana,* following the opening song and dance—four consecutive *Parivarta* circles, all accompanied by song, *Utthāpanī Dhruvā,* with a short break at the end of each *Parivarta* to renew in a much higher tempo.

The basic description of *Pūrvaraṅga* does not specify who was to circle the stage in the first *Parivarta*. It only says that it was performed slowly to the accompaniment of drums, silent in the other parts of *Utthāpana*. However, end of Chapter V specifies that "during the *Utthāpanī* [*Dhruvā*] when the *Parivarta* was made, [the stage] has been decorated with the flowers offered by the *Caturthakāra* (fourth performer) and [the theatre] resounded with the well-measured loud songs of expert musicians, divine drums should be played again and again" (*NŚ*.5.156-157). The cited *ślokas* mean the only moment of *Utthāpana,* at its very start, when the fourth performer taking part in the *Pūrvaraṅga* with the *Sūtradhāra* and his two assistants, appears on the empty stage to drumbeat. Evidently, he performed the first *Parivarta*, slow and flowing, accompanied by prolonged sounds of singing, as he circled the stage, spreading flowers all over it.

In the next *Parivarta*, the *Sūtradhāra* appeared simultaneously with his two assistants with handfuls of white flowers, one assistant carrying a gold jug, the other a *jarjara*—all three in white vestments. Before appearing on stage, they were to perform purifying rites, concentrate and put on amulets guarding off the evil spirits.

In a tentative interpretation of what followed, we can say that the initial part of the ceremony prepared the stage to sacrifice, the peak of the worship[22]. In the ritual context such activities meant to elevate the scenic action above the everyday reality of the profane world and give it a universal sacral meaning. In other words, the scenic space was to receive magical properties in a particular arrangement. As analyses of the *Nāṭyaśāstra* instructions show, the stage proceedings re-created the image of the world, making a ritual model of the Universe to translate the scenic space onto another, sacral cosmic scale. In the two initial stages of the *Pūrvaraṅga*—*Utthāpana* and *Parivartana*—the *Sūtradhāra* and his assistants created an order corresponding to the laws of the entire Universe. What they were doing was arranged in several interlinked stages.

According to the *Nāṭyaśāstra*, the *Sūtradhāra* started with Brahmā worship. Feet set slightly apart, he made five solemn steps in honour of the god and then several dancing steps simultaneously to his assistants. He stopped in the centre of the stage, close to the sacral point known as the *Brahmā-maṇḍala* (Brahmā's circle) to spread flowers over it as sacrifice to the god. This done, he pressed his hands together in the *Lalita* gesture and thrice bowed to Brahmā, every time making one step and touching the ground with his palms.

As we reconstrue the logics of the *Sūtradhāra*'s movements we can say that the sacralisation of the stage started with singling out its centre, ritually the most important point, symbol of the centre of the Universe materialized on the symbolical plane in the *Brahmā-maṇḍala*, where, according to the treatise, the god was present in person: "Brahmā himself occupied the centre of the stage, this is why flowers are scattered there" (*NŚ*.1.94; 5.74). By spreading flowers, the *Sūtradhāra* worshipped Brahmā, the supreme deity in the centre of the Universe, thus guaranteeing heavenly protection for the scenic ritual space.

According to the treatise, after he marked the centre and performed the Brahmā worship, the *Sūtradhāra* went over to the third *Parivarta* of the *Utthāpana*, the elevation of the *jarjara*, starting at a much quicker pace. He made a solemn circle with the centre in the *Brahmā-maṇḍala*, performing the *Pradakṣinā* with consecutive sequences of dancing steps, starting with the right foot, to which he pressed the left and the next step, the other way round. Next, he summoned an assistant with a gold jug of water for ablution, *Śauca*, and mouth rinsing in small gulps he had out of his palms (*Ācamana*), after which he again sprinkled water over his body—all this demanding an utmost zeal as purifying the *Sūtradhāra* for the ceremony, as the treatise had it. The ablution over, he reverentially took the *jarjara*, whose mission the *Nāṭyaśāstra* specified as removing all obstacles and elevated it, which meant the end of the third *Parivarta*, followed by an equally quick-paced fourth. As he said mantras, the *Sūtradhāra* made quick dancing steps, starting with the left foot, and then five special ritual steps backstage, toward the musical instruments, followed by another sequence of dancing steps. This was the end of the fourth *Parivarta* and, with it, the *Utthāpana* (*NŚ*.5.65-89).

Thus, according to the *Nāṭyaśāstra*, the stage of ritual space sacralisation which followed the emphatis is on the centre, was connected with the *jarjara* and its elevation. The book does not directly specify the religious symbolism of the *jarjara* and only mentions it as a heavenly weapon which protected the first drama from demons. Its ritual role is, however, easy to reconstrue. To all appearances, it was the principal vertical axis of the ritual space, associated with the symbolic axis of the imaginary world (*axis mundi*). In the symbolical structure of the rite the elevation of the *jarjara* must have been identical to that of the World Tree (*arboṛ mundi*), with similar semantics reflecting established links between all parts of the Universe and spelling the end of chaos[23]. The stage with its emphasised centre and vertical axis, presented a cosmogonic picture of the world, which necessitated a translation onto another, sacral temporal plane—an escape from the everyday, with its routine, into the rhythm of the universal movement. To all appearances, the *Pūrvaraṅga* achieved this translation through the vocal and instrumental accompaniment. The exceptional importance attached by the *Nāṭyaśāstra* to the music played throughout the *Pūrvaraṅga* makes us suggest that the tunes and songs had not so much an outer decorative as concrete ritual goal: they brought concord into the spatial and temporal characteristics of the cosmic model on stage. Most probably, the musical harmony gave an earthly manifestation to the cosmic order and protected the organized world from chaos. The music grew faster and faster with each *Parivarta* and ruled the performers' lightning movements, reflecting the rapid flow of cosmic time, simultaneously bringing harmony, dynamism and inner tension to the ritual space. Possibly, the very change of musical rhythm and tempo was seen as a way to make cosmic potentials more active as the rite awakened and supported them.

* * *

According to the *Nāṭyaśāstra*, when the *Utthāpana* was over, the *Sūtradhāra* went over to the next *Pūrvaraṅga* stage, the *Parivartana*, worship of the *Lokapālas*, keepers of the cardinal points. He moved with light, graceful steps round the stage, from right to left, making a large circle on it, accompanied by instruments and ritual song (*Parivartanī Dhṛuvā*) singing. After five ritual steps (*Atikrānta Cārī*), he stopped and bowed to the cardinal point corresponding to his position on the circle, then made another five, stopping for the next bow—first east, in honour of Indra, then south, in honour of Yama, west for Varuṇa and north for Dhanada (Kubera).

Evidently, his movements were symbolically meant to fix the border of the particular ritual space as coinciding with the border of the Universe, and delineate organized cosmos from chaos. This interpretation of the *Parivartana* is borne out by the entire logic of ritual proceedings, where the periphery came into the foreground after the centre was marked and vertical axis established. As the *Nāṭyaśāstra* testifies, the circle, with the centre in *Brahmā-maṇḍala*, was the protective and world-forming form in scenic rites—a large circle which delineated the sacral world from the profane and was also known as the *maṇḍala*, with four emphasised points oriented on the cardinal. As the *Sūtradhāra* made his round of the stage, he stopped in these points to bow to the *Lokapālas*, addressing them in their ritual function of world protectors and patrons of the basic geographical directions.

The *Nāṭyaśāstra* connected the following ascent of scenic sacrality with worship of the three supreme gods, Śiva, Brahmā and Viṣṇu, in neuter, male and female hypostases. The *Sūtradhāra* turned to face east and, with emphasised solemnity, performed three steps and bows, presented by the treatise as the 'male', the 'neuter' and the 'female', each in a different manner. The first, in worship of Śiva (Rudra), was with the raised right—'male'—leg; the next, Brahmā's, was with the moderately raised right, 'neuter', and the last, for Upendra (Viṣṇu), with the left, 'female' leg.

This performance must have ascended to the archaic mythology of the three steps with which Viṣṇu crossed all universal spheres and made the world one whole (RV.I.22.17; I.154). This is all the more probable since the *Sūtradhāra*'s worship of the three gods not merely brought order into the scenic space but made it one whole, protected in the centre and periphery, in the power of the three supreme deities who controlled all spheres of being. Orderly and integrated this space suited the climax of the rite—sacrifice. In keeping with *Nāṭyaśāstra* precepts, the fourth *Pūrvaraṅga* participant reappeared on stage, flowers in hand, moving to drumbeat and loud laudations (*stobha*) while the singers were silent. The fourth priest performed *pūjā*, flower offering, in honour of the *jarjara*, the *Sūtradhāra* and all musical instruments. The treatise did not describe his particular actions, but we can safely assume that he spread flowers at the *jarjara* foot, at the *Sūtradhāra*'s feet and on the floor before the instruments. The *pūjā* over, the priest left the stage to the protruded singing sounds of the *Apakṛṣṭā Dhruvā*.

As we see it, the sacral message of the *pūjā* signified the acquisition of supreme cosmic harmony, directly linked to the harmonization of the integrated scenic space, brought into order beforehand—to all appearances, through the special solemnity of ritual postures, music, measured movement and the beauty of white lotuses spread on the floor. During the *pūjā*, the performers were supposed to be the closest to the supra-personal world. The ritual replica of the Universe on the stage was considered merged with its cosmic prototype.

As the *Nāṭyaśāstra* had it the *pūjā* honoured the *jarjara*, the *Sūtradhāra* and the musical instruments. The book gave a mythological substantiation to *jarjara* worship—first, as the only ritual symbol visually present on stage. Second, according to the text, in "the sections (*parva*) [of the *jarjara*] the best and powerful gods were present. Brahmā occupied its topmost section, Śaṃkara (Śiva) the second, Viṣṇu the third section, Kārttikeya (Skanda) the fourth, and the great Nāgas—Śeṣa, Vāsukī and Takṣaka—the fifth" (*NŚ*.1.91-93). Thus, the very arrangement of the gods in the *jarjara* made it analogous to the *arbor mundi*, with the top in the highest divine spheres, and the roots reaching the underworld, ruled by the Nāgas, Great Serpents. As they performed the *pūjā* honouring the *jarjara*, the priests worshipped not merely the entire Universe, as embodied in the *axis mundi*, but gods embodied in the *jarjara*.

As the *pūjā* in the *Sūtradhāra*'s honour indicates, he personified a god at this ritual instance, as obliquely proved by the treatise mentioning the practice of *pūjā* dedication to a particular god. However, the stage had no special ritual symbol to be identified with a deity worshipped in the *pūjā*. Most probably, the *Sūtradhāra* assumed this part, as flowers were heaped at his feet. By communicating with the supra-personal world throughout the *Pūrvaraṅga*, he increased his own sacrality by posing as a visual embodiment of a god in the *pūjā*.

The worship of musical instruments—other *pūjā* objects—in the flower sacrifice clearly shows that the performers were aware of the key ritual function of music, as described above. As we can assume, not only the performers but the congregation perceived it, and the singing, as an earthly, aesthetised reflection of the divine element. The supreme spheric harmony sounded to all those present in the harmony of the chords.

* * *

But back to our description of the *Pūrvaraṅga*. The *pūjā* culminated it as the basic sacrament. Consequently, it was immediately followed by the Nāndī, the central litany of the scenic sacrifice, pronounced by the *Sūtradhāra* in logical correspondence with the ritual development. He appealed to the denizens of the divine space, whose attention the *Pūrvaraṅga* was attracting to this world and its affairs, for the well-being of the King, his realm, the priesthood and holy cows. The Nāndī runs as follows— after the *Nāṭyaśāstra* quotation: "Obeisance to all gods. Welfare unto the twice-born ones. May the King Soma be victorious. Let the cows attain good health. Let there be an advancement of the cause of the Brahmins and let their enemies be destroyed. Let the Mahārāja rule this earth with all the seas. May this realm prosper. Let this stage (spectacle) flourish and the *Prekṣākartṛ* (sponsor of the play) receive the great piety (*dharma*) given by Brahmā, who arranged it. Let the author of this drama (lit. composer of the *kāvya*) attain fame, and let his piety increase. May the deities be always pleased with this sacrifice" (*NŚ*.5.108-112). Both assistants of the *Sūtradhāra* loudly and clearly articulated, "Be it so for ever!" at the end of each *pada* of the *Nāndī* (*NŚ*.5.112-113).

A *Śuṣkāpakṛṣṭā Dhruvā*, ritual song, followed the *Nāndī*, and immediately after it, the *Sūtradhāra* loudly recited a *śloka* couplet, praising the god to whom the preceding *pūjā* was dedicated and the King or Brahmins (*NŚ*.5.116). The treatise does not directly indicate which of the gods shall be worshipped with a *pūjā*—certainly, not because a negligent compiler left it out. On the contrary, all ritual precepts are extremely precise in every detail. Besides, all information directly bearing on the *pūjā* is of extreme importance. So we can safely assume that flower sacrifices concerned all deities of the Hindu pantheon. This is highly plausible, considering the vague *Nāṭyaśāstra* indications of the *pūjā*-worshipped god and the absence of particular directions, to say nothing of the name. The ritual viewpoint also bears out this assumption, as the possibility to dedicate the *pūjā* to any god made its ritual goals extremely variegated and—even more important—guaranteed a universal ritual character of the *Pūrvaraṅga* as a whole.

The sacrificial sacrament was considered complete after the *pūjā* was performed and the *Nāndī* recited. The ceremonial rite was to proceed to a decline after the climax. With the *Pūrvaraṅga* goal attained, whatever the *Sūtradhāra* and his assistants did next was meant to desacralise the scenic space and divest it of ritual functions. The stage cosmic model was to be destroyed to rule out ill-intentioned or accidental impacts on the Universe. Importantly, the desacralisation of the ritual site is as essential and logically conditioned as its initial arrangement, and we find it in the ritual practices of many religions in varied forms.

The symbolic destruction of cosmos, acted out with its scenic model, started with the *Raṅgadvāra*, the ceremony of *jarjara* deposition. As the *Nāṭyaśāstra* testifies, the *Sūtradhāra* stayed on his own in the centre of the sacrificial site, as both his assistants receded backstage. *Aḍḍitā Dhruvā*, a ritual song, accompanied this solemn deposition, and the *jarjara-śloka* was recited to extol Indra's banner staff, followed by another *śloka* in honour of the deposition proper, which symbolized the deposition of the *arbor mundi*. Devoid of its vertical axis, the sacral world still survived, though partly robbed of harmony, stability and integrity.

With the *jarjara* in his right hand, the *Sūtradhāra* went over to the next *Pūrvaraṅga* stage, the *Cārī*, making five similar steps and a sequence of dancing steps with the left foot in the *Avahitta Sthāna* posture, his left hand performing the *Pallava* gesture. The movement completed, he stopped to recite a *Cārī-śloka* couplet, supposed to move the congregation to the *Śṛṅgāra Rasa*, emotional response. Next, he made another circle of the stage and receded backstage, back first, to hand the *jarjara* to an assistant and go over to the last and decisive stage of desacralisation, accompanied by quick-tempo singing. In a highly characteristic manner, the priest started with the movements prescribed for the next stage, the *Mahācārī*, with rapid steps now backstage, now forestage, again and again changing the steps and their rhythm and tempo. The initial dancing steps, directed towards the instruments, were followed by five quick steps with the left foot, feet always apart at the same distance, and a dancing step sequence, also with the left foot; then three steps forward in a different direction, and the dancing sequence repeated. Stopping after this, feet pressed close, the *Sūtradhāra* recited the *Raudra Rasa śloka,* the verse invoking fear in the congregation, and made three more ritual steps.

These enigmatic movements might seem disorderly but for the *Dhruvā* which disclosed their meaning. The *Nāṭyaśāstra* mentions this song as canonical and indispensable at this *Pūrvaraṅga* stage—a prayer and incantation, which included the following words: "Let this *Tāṇḍava* dance of Hara (Śiva) ever-beneficial, which smashed the hills by the impact of his sole and agitated the ocean with all creatures therein protect you at the time of the destruction of the world (*Pralaya*)" (*NŚ*.5.130-131).

Thus, as he performed the *Mahācārī,* the *Sūtradhāra* was likened unto Śiva in the performance of his orgiastic dance before the congregation. The ritual song and energetic movements must have produced a strong and consistent impression to impose a precise mythological parallel on the minds of those present: with his *Tāṇḍava* dance, Śiva destroyed the Universe, while the *Sūtradhāra* was destroying its sacral scenic image. All steps performed, the *Sūtradhāra* stood motionless while he recited the *Raudra Rasa śloka,* the verse of horror in keeping with the solemn moment at which harmony was lost.

This ritual and mythological interpretation of the *Cārī* and *Mahācārī* is borne out by the *Nāṭyaśāstra,* which points out that both these *Pūrvaraṅga* stages were, in times immemorial, performed by Maheśvara (Śiva) and Umā with diversified movements and *Rasas* (*NŚ*.5.122-123). The treatise connects the *Cārī* with Umā—Śiva's wife in her good and benevolent hypostasis and, even more important, the manifestation of her consort's creative urge—*śakti.* In its turn, the *Mahācārī* is directly associated with Śiva posing as Naṭarāja, the universal destroyer at the end of the cosmic death—*pralaya.*

As we see it, *Cārī* and *Mahācārī* can be seen as two parts of one ritual dance, in which Śiva's energy changes from light and creation to darkness and destruction. The entire congregation was supposed to precisely understand the subtle ritual content of the *Sūtradhāra*'s performance. This understanding was attained through a unique form of suggestion which the *Nāṭyaśāstra* called *rasa.* According to the treatise, the *Śṛṅgāra*

Rasa and *Raudra Rasa* were part and parcel of *Cārī* and *Mahācārī*, just as the songs and dances in it. More than that, not only the dancing postures but both *rasas* were invented by Umā and Śiva, as he first danced the *Tāṇḍava*. To understand the *rasa* as part of the analysed *Pūrvaraṅga* stages, we have to go into more detail on both its varieties.

The *Śṛṅgāra Rasa* was to emerge first, as connected with the *Cārī*. Traditionally seen as aesthetic perception of erotic emotions, as evoked by dramatic performance, to all appearances, it acquired this content rather recently. The earlier, original concept of this *Rasa* was connected with the idea of light, brilliance and chastity (*NŚ*.6, p.84)[24]. Possibly, when the *Sūtradhāra* performed the *Pūrvaraṅga*, his movement, mimicry and musical accompaniment were meant to evoke a feeling of light, grace and purity, rather than erotic emotions, inexplicable and out of place in this context. Significantly, the *Nāṭyaśāstra* connects the *Cārī* pantomime with Umā, whose name means 'light', 'purity', 'grace'. Most probably, as he suggested *Śṛṅgāra Rasa* with his entire performance, the *Sūtradhāra* imposed on his congregation the feeling of an ideal and perfectly harmonious Universe imbued with radiant light[25]. The recital of the *Cārī-śloka*, the couplet also invoking *Śṛṅgāra Rasa*, brought this mass suggestion to a climax with its unique word combinations. The light and joy perceived by the worshippers crowned the manifestations of the divine element, omnipotent ruler of the harmonious Universe.

The *Cārī* over, the destruction of the ordered cosmos started, next to go over to a chaotically indefinite and disintegrated world. As the *Sūtradhāra* performed the *Mahācārī*, he was not merely to symbolically destroy the sacral scenic space but to actualize a totally different feeling, which he suggested to the whole congregation. The luminous *Śṛṅgāra Rasa* gave way to the dark and awesome *Raudra Rasa*, intrinsically linked to Śiva, its divine patron (*NŚ*.6.44). The entire expressive idiom of the rite was used to create this impression—quicker tunes, and harsh and angular movements of the *Sūtradhāra*, as against his previous flowing steps and gestures. Cosmic light gave way to the darkness of chaos—a sensation precisely expressed in *Raudra Rasa* verses. In fact, the perception of every *Rasa*, a sophisticated and independent ritual device within the *Pūrvaraṅga*, gave the congregation a supra-personal and ecstatic awareness of being part of the divine element and a knowledge of God in his radiant hypostasis of Creator and Protector of the World, and the fearsome, of the Universal Destroyer[26].

* * *

Let us now get back to our description of the rite. Evidently, the *Sūtradhāra* was alone on stage as the ritual space was destroyed: the *Nāṭyaśāstra* mentions him summoning his assistants, who appeared accompanied by ritual song, *Narkuṭaka Dhruvā*, to which the *Sūtradhāra* performed dancing steps with his left foot. Possibly, his assistants had changed their attire while out of stage, judging by the fact that one of them reappeared as *Vidūśaka*, a bald dwarfish hunchback, making the congregation laugh. All performers again took their places on stage, and the next *Pūrvaraṅga* stage started—the *Trigata*—as the *Nāṭyaśāstra* had it, a concise costume interlude "in the form of a play" (*NŚ*.5.139). In the *Trigata* the performers "played at hints" with an exchange of obscure questions like,"Who stands [here]?" or "Who has won?" and equally obscure elliptic answers. *Vidūśaka*'s speech was the darkest, full of incoherent phrases which made the *Sūtradhāra* smile (*NŚ*.5.138).

The *Trigata* is traditionally interpreted as a ritual exchange of riddles, not unlike the Vedic verbal duels[27]. We do not reject this interpretation, but think it necessary to make it more concrete. As we see it, its ritual function was directly linked with the *Mahācārī* destruction of the ritual space. This viewpoint is borne out by the *Nāṭyaśāstra* definition: "The *Trigata* shall be performed in the *Bhāratī*. The *Vidūśaka* should utter a discourse consisting of the same but mostly incoherent words causing the *Sūtradhāra* to smile. [This manner] becomes the controversial topic (*Vitaṇḍā*), structured as a play, with abrupt remarks (*Gaṇḍa*), enigmatical allusions (*Nālikā*) and [questions as] 'Who stands [here]?', 'Who has won?', etc." (*NŚ*.5.137-139).

As we analyse this definition, let us centre our attention first on the demand to perform the *Trigata* with the help of *Bhāratī*, where, beyond doubt, the *Bhāratī Vṛtti* is meant—one of the four ancient Indian theatrical styles, combining versatile devices used by actors to re-create the actuality on stage[28]. As the *Nāṭyaśāstra* has it, the word was the main expressive means of the *Bhāratī Vṛtti*, dominating over other kinds of scenic representation in this style (*NŚ*.22.25). In the *Trigata*, however, the *Sūtradhāra*, *Vidūśaka* and the second assistant not merely exchanged retorts but spoke exaltedly (*NŚ*.20.128), and their abrupt remarks (*Gaṇḍa*) followed from arguments which started because of their excitement, irritation, verbosity and mutual reproaches (*NŚ*.20.129). Thus, according to the definition, the *Trigata* was an expressive verbal exchange, a stormy debate dominated by *Vidūśaka* and the second assistant.

Notably, the verbal duel characteristic of the *Bhāratī Vṛtti* in the *Trigata* is mythologically based on the *Nāṭyaśāstra* legend about the divine origin of the four styles. We shall retell it in detail as it reveals the ritual message of the *Trigata* in the *Pūrvaraṅga*. As the *Pralaya* finished, turning the Universe into an Ocean, and Viṣṇu, mighty keeper of the world, reclined on a serpent in its midst, *Asuras* Madhu and Kaiṭabha approached him intoxicated with their power and challenged the god. In the battle that followed, the fighters struck and kicked, and showered each other with torrential abuse, so that the Universe shook all over. As he heard the frenzied expletives, Brahmā ordered Viṣṇu to kill the two brawlers as soon he could, and noted the advent of the articulated speech, *Bhāratī Vṛtti*, which spelt the rebirth of the world in a new state. In his reply, Viṣṇu said that he had made *Bhāratī Vṛtti* among other weapons as the strongest, which enabled him to conquer the *Asuras* (*NŚ*.22.1-10). In fact, the myth presents an episode on which rests another cycle of Creation. Here, the re-emerging activity of the Universal creative forces, which survive the *Pralaya* as mere potentials, is directly linked with the genesis of speech.

Its hard to say whether the legend mythologically explained what was taking place in the *Trigata*, or the myth and the rite both appealed to a shared source of the picture of the Universe as the embodied Logos. The connection between the legend of the birth of *Bhāratī Vṛtti* and the *Trigata* is, however, beyond doubt, as shown by the entire talk—a chain of riddles and incidental remarks. We see much of what happens in the *Trigata* as obscure and mysterious mainly because we need precise knowledge of the ritual and mythological context, if we are to correctly understand these riddles and hints. Most probably, the bulk of the congregation possessed of this knowledge and fully understood the *Trigata* events as more than disinterested spectators. Probably, they saw it as developing on the same mythological theme of the Universal state at the end of the *Pralaya*, when after the destruction of the cosmos with the *Tāṇḍava* dance and obliteration of its scenic sacral image in the rite a balance sets in, and things sleep in waiting for another rebirth. In the cyclic time of mythic history, as reflected in the legend of the birth of *Bhāratī Vṛtti*, the *Pralaya* is followed by all living things coiled up onto the seed, and the Universe turns into an Ocean under Viṣṇu's divine protection. However, the *Trigata* proceeds in its ritual scenic space, considerably desacralised by the *Mahācārī*, which destructed an ordered cosmic model on the stage. Besides, the *Trigata* takes place at a troubled time like what followed the *Pralaya*. If the triumph of divinity and light is evident in a whole and harmonious Universe, then the myth of Viṣṇu's victory and the *Trigata* events were meant, as we see it, to put an end to all doubt of the omnipotence of the divinity in an inert, non-developing cosmos.

If this ritual interpretation of the *Trigata* is correct, evidently, the *Sūtradhāra* was identified as Brahmā, his assistant as Viṣṇu, and the repulsive *Vidūśaka* as the *Asuras*. Thus the verbal duel of the assistant and *Vidūśaka* re-created Viṣṇu's mythic battle with the demons, in which *Bhāratī Vṛtti* emerged in times immemorial. The speech of assistant in Viṣṇu's part symbolized the Word, counterpoised to the incoherent words of *Vidūśaka*, doomed to be smitten, like the *Asuras*, who broke the Universal peace. The exchange of hints and incidental retorts was probably clear to the enlightened. They knew precise answers to who was on stage and who the victor. This reconstruction of the ritual and mythological role of the *Trigata* not merely corresponds to the overall logic of *Pūrvaraṅga* progress but sheds light on the dark etymology of the word *Vidūśaka*, which means 'brawler', 'desecrator', 'foul-mouth', etc.[29].

Thus, the *Mahācārī* symbolized final destruction of the scenic space, while the *Trigata* showed its potential revival in a new cosmic cycle. What happened next had no Universal content but bore a local message. The final *Pūrvaraṅga* part, *Prarocanā*, was not a divine worship—the *Nāṭyaśāstra* sets the *pūjā* limits between the *Pratyāhāra* and *Mahācārī* (*NŚ*.5.55)—but it was connected with the drama closer than any previous stage. In particular, the *Prarocanā* mentions a play plot to provide conditions for its good performance. We can't say now whether it was considered less sacral than the other stages, but its different ritual functions are doubtless. First of all, the *Prarocanā* was meant to guarantee divine protection for the *Nāṭya* played right after the *Pūrvaraṅga*.

* * *

We have described the basic *Pūrvaraṅga* stages and reconstrued the logic of ritual events. Now we ought to regard the cult function of the rite as a whole. We know the *Pūrvaraṅga* from a treatise on drama, and so it is traditionally seen as a conventional prologue to a drama, meant solely to consecrate it. This function of a long and complicated rite is doubtless, but hardly the only. Characteristically, the *Nāṭyaśāstra* never directly alludes to the *Pūrvaraṅga* as the rite consecrating a play, but repeatedly stresses its status as a liturgy in *pūjā* form. To quote the treatise, the *Pūrvaraṅga* "should be a *pūjā* to gods and is a *pūjā* to gods and is conducive of *dharma*, fame and longevity" (*NŚ*.5.57). The drama proper was separated from the *Pūrvaraṅga*—more than that, non-obligatory, as far as the inner ritual logic was concerned. In other words, it did not matter so much whether a play followed it or not. The ritual events were important for themselves.

In fact, of all *Pūrvaraṅga* stages, the *Prarocanā* alone had a direct connection with the drama as a transition to it from the rite. But then, it lay outside the symbolical sequence of ritual proceedings which made up the *pūjā* and could not be reduced to the idea of religious elevation of the *Nāṭya*. As we see it, the *Pūrvaraṅga*, as appealing to a wealth of Hindu myths, was universal and autonomous enough—a cyclic liturgy which demanded regular re-enactment and, in the ritual typological aspect, resembled nothing closer than Christian liturgies. As a regular rite, it not so much preluded or consecrated a drama as worshipped gods in a specific form, the *pūjā*, accompanied with a *Nāṭya*. In this sense, the *Pūrvaraṅga-Nāṭya* correlation is typologically comparable to the relation between the liturgy and the liturgical drama, which existed in the Christian ecclesiastical practice.

* * *

To sum up this analysis of the *Pūrvaraṅga*, we can't but think about its performers—persons capable of flawless reproduction of long and complicated rites, and endowed with the necessary esoteric knowledge. The *Nāṭyaśāstra* repeatedly refers to Brahmins debating the *Nāṭya* and *Nāṭyaveda*, who address its legendary father, Bharata Muni, with questions at the beginning of every chapter. Many prayers and incantations are said for the well-being of the priesthood. Indications in the treatise make us assume that the *Nāṭya* was the lot of Brahmins. They were the first to enact a drama on stage at Brahmā's bidding, and they preserve and pass on the sacral knowledge of the *Nāṭyaveda*. As we can safely suggest, the *Pūrvaraṅga* was also enacted by Brahmins, excellent professionals with special training. The *Pūrvaraṅga* involved four male priests, with the *Sūtradhāra* as leader. If they participated on their own, the *Pūrvaraṅga* was termed *Śuddha*, pure. It easily turned into a *Citra*, decorated, by involving female dancers dressed as celestial maidens and acting goddesses. They appeared only once, at the start of the rite, after its fourth participant spread white flowers on the stage (*NŚ*.5.158-162). Chapter IV gives a detailed description of the ceremony preceding the dance. At first, only one dancer appeared with a bunch of flowers, to staccato drumbeat, assumed the ritual posture, *Vaiśakha Sthāna*, and made four canonical movements, *Recaka*, involving her whole body and followed by a round of the stage, on which she spread flowers to form a *maṇḍala*. After this divine worship came bows in honour of the gods, and a small mis-en-scene, in which the girl retold the simultaneous song in gestures and movements (*abhinaya*), next giving place to a group of dancing girls, who performed a solemn dance (*NŚ*.4.276-282).

Thus, the *Pūrvaraṅga* had a longer (*Caturasra*) and shorter (*Tryasra*) versions, and included either men alone or men and women. A description of every stage and reconstruction of the ritual sequence allow us to conclude that it was a sophisticated rite with well-developed semantics and a subtle symbolic system.

THE RITE OF THE THEATRE FOUNDATION

Unlike the *Pūrvaraṅga*, two other *Nāṭyaśāstra* rites were directly related with the construction and consecration of theatres, and performed only once in every building. Chapter II of the treatise describes the first as a long ritual ceremony with tremendous religious consequences, to be performed in the light of *Mūlā* star[30], on the most propitious day of the month, determined by Brahmins after they received generous donations. The rite started with the measurement of the construction site with a rope sprinkled with holy water. Connected with a wealth of omens, it demanded the utmost care. The rope tearing in two during the work portended death to the theatre patron, in three internecine strife in the country, and in four, death to a priest with stage education (*NŚ*.2.28-31). If the workers dropped the rope, other dire results were expected.

The site measured and levelled out, the foundation was laid to the sound of percussion and other instruments. Courtesans, persons clad in dark-red, cripples and *Śramaṇas*, were driven off the site for the ceremony (*NŚ*.2.37-38). Sacrifice of incense, flowers, fruit and ritual food—*Bali*—was made with the nightfall, arranged in ten directions in honour of the gods protecting them. The sacrifices to the four cardinal points were to have obligatory colourings—white for the east, blue west, yellow south and red north, with mantras recited in honour of the patrons of all four points. Brahmins also received *ghee*, purified melted butter, and *Pāyasa*[31], the King—*Madhuparka*[32], and *Nāṭya* experts—treacled rice (*NŚ*.2.41-42).

The soil was levelled and ploughed with particular care for the stage—the heart of the playhouse—with the plough drawn by two white unblemished draught animals. Black earth cleaned of pebbles and grass was brought next. The work was done by persons without the slightest bodily flaw. Gems and precious metals were put in the stage foundation, a diamond to the east side, lapis lazuli south, quartz west, coral north, and gold in the centre (*NŚ*.2.69-74).

All parts of the building marked and foundation laid, construction started on the walls. This completed, columns were erected on another auspicious night, in the starlight of *Rohiṇī* or *Śravaṇā*[33]. Apart from supporting the roof, the columns had a ritual function. Four of the many were specially important as oriented on points midway between the cardinal to symbolize the basic *varṇas*—Brahmins, Kṣatriyas, Vaiśyas and Śūdras. A priest opened the ceremony at the break of the appointed day after a three-day fast, marking the spot for every column with sacrificial garlands of green leaves, with incantations of the *Svasti* ("Let it be good") and *Puṇyāha* ("Let it be an auspicious day") types (*NŚ*.2.54).

A symbolic colour corresponded to each of the four columns to determine the four changes of attire and colour of sacrifices. The Brahmin pillar rose the first to the accompaniment of many musical instruments, with all participants clad in white, and to the following mantra: "Just as Mount Meru is unshakable and the Himalayas remain firm, also be thou unshakable and bring victory to the King" (*NŚ*.2.61-62). *Pāyasa* was distributed between all Brahmins present while the pillar was erected.

The next, Kṣatriya pillar, demanded priests arrayed in red, with bright red sacrificial garlands and ointments. Another canonical mantra was recited as the pillar rose and all twice-born got treacled rice.

The northwest, Vaiśya pillar, with its yellow symbols, was erected by yellow-clad priests, who read the appropriate mantra and received rice with *ghee*. The last, northeast, for Śūdras, required dark raiments, and all twice-born received *Kṛsarā*[34] to the sounds of another mantra.

All pillars erected, they were to be honoured with prescribed sacrifices. Gold, and white ointments and flower garlands were laid at the foot of the Brahmin pillar, copper of the Kṣatriya, silver Vaiśya and iron Śūdra. Gold was put at the foot of all other columns. The ceremony implied sumptuous donations to Brahmins—jewellery, rich garments and cows (*NŚ*.2.54)[35]. The *Nāṭyaśāstra* specifies a cow as the best reward for the Brahmin pillar erected. The other *varṇa* pillars demanded a feast for all priests and builders involved, with all dishes blessed in advance with mantras read over them by a *Nāṭyācārya*, priest expert on the theatre. The Chief Priest and the King also were gifted honey and *Pāyasa*, and all the rest *Kṛsarā* and salt (*NŚ*.2.58-60).

All these rich gifts guaranteed divine patronage to the pillars. Their erection was a highly responsible task: if they shook, turned or moved otherwise, these were omens of drought, famine and enemy invasion (*NŚ*.2.55-57).

Similar ceremonies accompanied the building of all walls and dressing rooms, and door hinging (*NŚ*.2.60-63). The building of *Mattavāraṇīs*, side stage elevations, also required special rites, with flower garlands, incense and particularly coloured garments sacrificed, and ritual dishes, of the *Pāyasa* and *Kṛsarā* types, distributed. Stage building crowned the construction, after which the edifice was decorated and considered completed.

THE RITE OF THE THEATRE CONSECRATION

The construction completed, the *Nāṭyaśāstra* demanded the consecration of the new theatre in a rite lasting many days. To prepare the building for the ceremony, cows and Brahmins were to spend seven days in it, the latter quietly reciting mantras, to liken the edifice unto a dwelling. The week over, the *Nāṭyācārya* started the rite. "He has been initiated for the purpose and has clad in new raiments. Previously the *Nāṭyācārya* should have observed fast for three days and have kept his senses under control. He should have desisted from lying in comfortable bedsteads during those days of fast. After he has become purified, will he sprinkle his limbs with water over which purificatory mantras have been muttered" (*NŚ*.3.2-4). Next he was to spend a night in the theatre, worshipping many gods. His first prayer was addressed to *Bhava* (Śiva), great god and sovereign of the worlds, the next to Brahmā, who sprung from the lotus, and the third to Viṣṇu. The worship of the three supreme gods was followed by addresses to Indra, Guha (Skanda), the goddesses Sarasvatī, Lakṣmī, Siddhi (Luck), Medhā (Wisdom), Smṛti (Memory), Mati (Prayer), *Soma* and Sūrya, and then the *Maruts, Lokapālas, Aśvins, Mitra, Agni, Rudras, Varṇa* gods, *Kāla, Kali, Mṛtyu* (Death) and *Niyati* (Reticence). Then came the turn of *Kāla*'s sceptre, Viṣṇu's weapon,

Vāsuki the lord of the Nāgas, *Vajra* (Indra's divine mace), *Vidyut* (Lightning), Seas, *Gandharvas*, *Apsaras*, *Muni* (Sage), *Nāṭyakumārīs*, *Mahāgrāmaṇīs* (village protectresses), *Yakṣas*, *Guhyakas* and *Bhūta* hosts (*NŚ*.3.3-8).

This worship attracted divine attention to the new abode of the *Nāṭya*. After long prayers, the *Nāṭyācārya* made an *añjali*, praying gesture, and summoned the gods to their seats in the theatre: "This night, you shall help and protect us and those who will come after us in this *Nāṭya*" (*NŚ*.3.9-10).

The nighttime part of the ceremony also included worship of musical instruments, prelude to the *pūjā* in honour of Indra's banner staff. "After all gods and musical instruments have been worshipped, a *pūjā* in honour of the *jarjara* shall be performed for the acquisition of grand success for the *Nāṭya*" (*NŚ*.3.11). The prescribed sacrifice to the *jarjara* over, the *Nāṭyācārya* started a *pūjā* in all gods' honour at daybreak, "in the starlight of *Ārdrā*, *Maghā* or *Yāmyā*, or three luminaries deserving of worship, or *Aśleṣā* and *Mūlā*"[36] (*NŚ*.3.15), the stage flooded with lamplight. The *pūjā* was not performed before the *Ācārya* purified his body, concentrated his mind on the rite, and initiated himself.

The next stage of the ceremony started only at sunset, "at the concluding moment of the day, a time trying and fearsome, full of evils and mighty *Bhūtas*" (*NŚ*.3.17), when the *Nāṭyācārya* performed the *Ācamana*, rinsing his mouth with water taken from his palms in small portions, and went over to the rite termed "the installation of gods" in the treatise (*NŚ*.3.17). It enumerates all rules "in accordance with which all the gods are to be installed in their conventional form and colours in their respective positions" (*NŚ*.3.32). This rite started with the *Nāṭyācārya* drawing the *maṇḍala* in the proper spot of the stage floor, in which he followed these directions: "Measure 16 *hastas*[37] along the perimeter of the *maṇḍala*, where the doors shall be made [facing] the four cardinal points according to the rules, with two upward diagonals in the centre of the resultant arch. In the apartments made by these lines different deities are installed" (*NŚ*.3.21-22). As he divided his careful drawing of the *maṇḍala* in eight, the *Nāṭyācārya* oriented this mystic diagram of the Universe on the cardinal and midway points, after which he arranged the gods.

Brahmā, who had lotus as his seat, was the first to take his place in the centre of the *maṇḍala*. The eight sectors were filled next, starting with the east, the holiest point, the abode of *Bhava* (Śiva) with *Bhūta* hosts, Nārāyaṇa (Viṣṇu), Indra, Skanda, Arka (*Sūrya*), the *Aśvins*, *Candra*, Sarasvatī, Lakṣmī, Śraddhā and Medhā. Next came southeast, with *Agni* and *Svāhā*, Viśvedevas, *Gandharvas*, *Rudras* and *Ṛsi* (Sages). Then, south, with *Yama* and *Mitra* with their retinue, *Pitṛs*, *Piśācas*, *Uragas* and *Guhyakas*, and southwest, with *Rākṣasas* and all *Bhūtas*. The west sector belonged to Varuṇa and the Seas; northwest to the Seven Winds and Garuḍa with other birds; north to Dhanada (Kubera), the *Nāṭyamatṛkā* goddesses, *Yakṣas* and *Guhyakas*; and northeast to *Nandī*, *Gaṇa* lords, *Brahmarṣi* and *Bhūta* hosts. Thus the *Nāṭyācārya* filled all *maṇḍala* sectors, and appealed to four more gods to settle in the pillars round the stag—Sanatkumāra east, Dakṣa south, Grāmaṇī north, and Skanda west.

The gods placed on stage, incense, garlands and unguents were to be sacrificed to them. All received white ointments and white flower garlands, with the exception of *Agni*, *Gandharvas* and *Sūrya*, entitled to red sacrifices. After this, the culmination of the ceremony came with the start of the second *pūjā*, which used plant seeds, *Nāgapuṣpa* powder, husked saffron, various foods, and red fruit and flowers. Everything used in the flower sacrifice was to have the aroma of red sandalwood.

Proceeding from the treatise, we can thus reconstrue the *Ācārya*'s performance in this *pūjā* within the theatre consecration rite. He started his worship in the *maṇḍala* centre, where Brahmā was seated in a lotus. Approaching this point, the priest placed *Madhuparka*, sacrificial food, in it with the following prayer: "O God of Gods, thou of a glorious destiny, *Pitāmaha* born in the lotus, take our oblation purified by the mantra" (*NŚ*.3.46).

Śiva, the next object of worship, received sweets with the following laudatory mantra: "O God of Gods, great god Gaṇeśa (Śiva), thou who ended the Tripura, accept this oblation purified by the mantra, O God prosperous in *māyā* " (*NŚ*.3.47).

Viṣṇu also received sacrificial sweets with this mantra: "O Nārāyaṇa, whose ways are not to be measured, O Padmanābha, the best of all gods, receive this oblation purified by the mantra" (*NŚ*.3.48).

The other deities were worshipped likewise, with hymns and bows—Sarasvatī with *Pāyasa*, Indra with sweets, *Agni* boiled rice with baked milk, *Soma* and *Sūrya* treacle, *Gandharvas* and *Munis* honeyed *Pāyasa*, *Yama* and *Mitra* cakes and sweets, *Varuṇa Pāyasa* with baked milk, *Pitṛs*, *Piśācas* and *Uragas* milk and melted butter, *Bhūta* and *Rākṣasa* hosts roast and boiled meat, wine (*surā*), nectar, peas in milk, and fruit, *Dānavas* wine and meat, and the rest cakes, *Utkarikā* and boiled rice. Thus the *Ācārya* stepped east to west, stopping in every *maṇḍala* sector to honour the gods with *pūjā* (*NŚ*.3.33-71).

The second *pūjā* over, another part of the ceremony set in, practically unconnected with the previous and, presumably, preceded by cleaning the stage of all its paraphernalia except the *maṇḍala*. Now, a jar, *kumbha*, full of water was placed in its centre, with a gold piece inside and a green leaf garland sacrificed to it. The musical instruments now remained silent, covered with special cloth. The rite that followed repeated the sequence described above—another sacrifice of incense, garlands, flowers and food in the third *pūjā*, centered on the worship of the instruments, all gods and the *jarjara*.

The latter, consecrated with a particular rite, was brought to the ritual space and decorated with multicoloured cloth pieces on stage. The top, Brahmā's abode, was tied with white, Śiva's below with blue, Viṣṇu yellow, Skanda red and the *Nāgas*, at the bottom, motleycoloured. A special mantra then performed the consecration sacrament as the gods were invoked one by one to take their places in the *jarjara* and give it a sacral power by their patronage. From this instance on, the *jarjara* became the sacred weapon of all gods and was to bring the King victories and prosperity (*NŚ*.3.72-81).

After this *pūjā*, the priest went over to the next part of the rite. Unlike the traditional scenic rites of instrument, god and *jarjara* worship, this was unprecedented and had no parallel in any of the rites specified by the *Nāṭyaśāstra*. It started with the *Homa*, when *havis*, purified melted butter, was poured into the sacred fire to the sounds of a special mantra. A flaming brazier must have appeared on stage for the purpose, though the treatise never mentions it.

A crucial moment followed, when the King appeared on stage with dancing girls, and the solemn rite *Parimārjana* was performed to purify him as the *Ācārya* honoured him, the dancers and the instruments with burning logs—surely, taken from the brazier—to purify the performers, which was the core of this rite, and enhance their glory and sanctity (*NŚ*.3.82-83). He next sprinkled them with water blessed with a mantra and addressed them with this incantation meant for the King's luck: "Thou wert born into a grand family and endowed with many virtues from birth, and since they are inborn, may they abide with thee forever" (*NŚ*.3.84-85), to be followed by a prayer for the success of the *Nāṭya*. In fact, he invoked its mother goddesses for ritual protection of the King and dancers: "May all these Mothers—Sarasvatī, Dhṛti, Medhā, Hrī, Śrī, Lakṣmī and Smṛti—protect ye and make ye affluent" (*NŚ*.3.86-87).

This prayer was followed with another *Homa*, with a mantra recited and purified melted butter poured into the fire, ending the ceremony which demanded royal participation and was framed with two libations.

The precepts on this score are too concise to see whether the King and dancers were to remain on stage afterwards. Even if they left, what followed was connected with the King in its prophetic symbolism. After the *Homa*, the priest was to perform the *Kumbhabhedana*, breaking the jar with the utmost care. The success of this rite guaranteed the King's martial victories. If, on the contrary, the vessel remained whole, this foreboded defeat and the enemy's passing triumph. Next came the *Raṅgapradīpana*, when the *Ācārya* made a running circle of the stage, burning *Dīpa* oil-lamp in hand, with little jumps, finger snapping and as much noise as he could make.

The final stage of the royal rite, also with a prophetic content, is described very dryly and concisely. Silent to this moment, the musical instruments, mainly percussion, now accompanied a battle scene. The treatise does not specify the number of performers involved, nor their weapons, nor whether it was a pantomimical make-believe or real fighting. Only the closing *śloka* mentions accidental wounds as a good omen if they are deep and amply bleed, promising success to all later ventures (*NŚ*.3.91-93). The end of the fighting scene closed the theatre consecration ceremony. Built according to the rules and consecrated by *pūjā*, the edifice was ready for the *Pūrvaraṅga* and *Nāṭya*.

* * *

The consecration ceremony proper comprised three consecutive rites, each with a message and ritual goal all its own. The first, started at night and finished at daybreak, sanctified the whole edifice, treated as an integral sacral space. Whatever the *Ācārya* was doing—his prayers to all gods and the final *pūjā*—had precise mythic correspondences. To give them this mythological interpretation, we must turn to Chapter I of the *Nāṭyaśāstra*, which describes the genesis of the drama and the divine origin of the theatre building.

Tradition tells of the first drama, about gods' victory over the *Asuras*—a plot hardly to demons' liking. "*Vighnas* [lit., troublemakers], accompanied by the *Asuras*, recurred to *māyā* (magical power) and paralyzed the speech, movement and memory of the dancer players" (*NŚ*.1.66). Indra, the first to come to rescue, repeated his feat in another battle with *Asuras*, piercing *Vighnas* and *Asuras*, crowded on stage, with his divine banner staff, *dhwaja*, which earned it the glory of drama protector and the name of *jarjara*, smashing to smithereens. But even this mighty weapon was unable to wholly protect the *Nāṭya*—enacted in the open, the drama was too vulnerable. The demons again attempted to thwart the performance. This time, Brahmā himself lent a merciful ear to Bharata's supplication and invented a universal way to protect the drama, a building known as the abode of the *Nāṭya*, and passed esoteric knowledge to divine architect Viśvakarman. "O highsouled one", Brahmā said to him. "Erect an edifice for the *Nāṭya*, endowed with all good qualities" (*NŚ*.1.79). When it was ready, Brahmā led Mahendra (Indra) and a few chosen of the best among the gods to see the building. "On seeing the playhouse, Brahmā said to all the gods: 'This edifice for the *Nāṭya* should be protected by you all taking up the responsibility of the different parts severally' " (*NŚ*.1.82).

According to divine will and volition, "the house as a whole is protected by *Candra*, in the cardinal points by the *Lokapālas*, and midway between them by the *Maruts*. *Mitra* is responsible for the dressing rooms, *Varuṇa* for the air within the building, *Agni* the shrine, and all celestial beings for musical instruments. The gods of the four *Varṇa*s shall protect the pillars, *Āditya*s and *Rudra*s the space within them; *Bhūta*s the banisters, *Apsara*s the rooms, *Yakṣiṇī*s all auxiliary premises, and the Sea God the earth surface underneath. *Yama* and *Kāla* shall be in charge of the doors and [other] premises. *Yama*'s sceptre protects the threshold, Śiva's spear the upper part of the door, while *Niyati* and *Mrtyu* stand guard to the sides of the door. Great Indra placed himself on the stage edge. The lightning, *Daitya*s' bane, was placed to guard the *Mattavāraṇī*, Brahmā himself occupied the stage centre, and *Yakṣa*s, *Guhyaka*s and *Piśāca*s, denizens of the underworld, are to protect the space under the stage" (*NŚ*.1.83-95).

This lengthy list allows us to see that the gods whom the *Ācārya* invoked to the new theatre almost wholly coincided with the ones whom Brahmā appointed protectors and guards of the world's first theatre. This observation is borne out by the *Ācārya*'s pronounced intention to call all gods without exception in his prayer—probably, a concealed appeal to this legend, which must have had a place of honour in the *Nāṭyaśāstra* mythological compendium as a genesis myth.

The *Ācārya* performed a unique ritual sacrament by invoking the gods to take their places in the theatre as indicated by Brahmā in times immemorial. Thus an earthly building received sacrality. The *Ācārya*'s ritual performance turned the theatre into a model of the Universe, where every god had the place determined for him.

The next parts of the rite followed the *Pūrvaraṅga* pattern, repeated in the majority of the *Nāṭyaśāstra* rites. It demanded the worship of musical instruments, *jarjara* and deities—the three principal objects of the *pūjā*. The worship of the instruments, which remained conspicuously silent in this part of the rite, stemmed from their high sacral status in this particular set of religious ideas. Characteristically, the legend of the first theatre construction emphasizes the particular status of instruments, pointing out that all gods without exception guard and protect them.

The *jarjara pūjā* evidently had the same semantics as the *pūjā* sacrifice in the *Pūrvaraṅga* though, as we see it, this part of the consecration rite laid special stress only on one aspect of the polysemantic symbolism of this crucial ritual object—its status as a magic weapon which in its time saved the *Nāṭya* from malicious *Vighnas*. To all appearances, this was the function of the *jarjara* in this rite—an interpretation borne out by the mantric incantation which accompanied the *pūjā* in honour of Indra's banner. The canonical mantra found in the *Nāṭyaśāstra* differs in content from other appeals to the *jarjara*. Doubtless, this text had a ritual meaning and was said only at this moment of the worship: "Thou art Mahendra's missile able to kill all the demons (*Dānavas*) and superbly created by all the gods; thou art capable of destroying all the obstacles [or *Vighnas*], bring victory to the King and defeat to his enemies, welfare unto cows and Brahmins, and steady progress to the art of *Nāṭya*" (*NŚ*.3.12-13). In fact, this mantra actualizes the ritual role of the *jarjara* which it played but once in theatrical history before the first abode of the *Nāṭya* was built, and which found reflection in the legend on the origin of the drama.

After the instrument and *jarjara* worship, the *Ācārya* started the *pūjā* in honour of all gods, as mythologically substantiated in the *Nāṭyaśāstra*, Chapter I. After he made the *Nāṭya* and built a theatre, Brahmā set the order for a cult ceremony without which no venture related to the drama could be started. "Pitāmaha (Brahmā) said to the gods: 'Perform duly a sacrifice in the playhouse with *Bali* offerings, *Homa*, *Mantras* and *Japas*, [sacred] herbs and *Naivedyas* [food offerings] which should consist of foodstuffs hard and soft' " (*NŚ*.1.123-124). Only "thus you all will have a happy *pūjā* in the world of the mortals" (*NŚ*.1.124).

The treatise relates the start of the construction of playhouses designed for the *pūjā* and *Nāṭya* to a very early stage in the evolution of the theatre, close to its origin. According to the above-quoted legend, the abode of the *Nāṭya* houses the first or at least second performance, preceded by the *pūjā*. In other words, the mythological time of the *Nāṭyaśāstra* combines three crucial events: the birth of the *Nāṭya*, the construction of the first theatre and a *pūjā* in it.

We could safely assume that the legendary narration of Chapter I has no historical background, and the indications to the sacral origin and sanctity of the playhouse are only meant to raise the status of the *Nāṭya*. However, this and other parts of the treatise, related to later stages in the drama evolution, never treat the theatre as a secular building intended to entertain the laity. Many rites described in the treatise are expressly meant for theatre consecration. A theatre is Brahmā's creation, an abode of gods and the site for *pūjā*—in other words, a purely sacral building analogous to a temple.

The *Nāṭyaśāstra* rites connected with the building and sanctification of a theatre are analogous to the rites of temple foundation and consecration in other religions with sophisticated church architecture[38]. There is another telling coincidence, regular special services in the theatre, typologically close to Christian liturgies—the *Pūrvaraṅga*, with its liturgical essence and regular stage repetitions.

To sum up the above, the *Nāṭyācārya* devoted the first part of the theatre consecration to its mystical protection. Through prayers and a *pūjā*, he created a unique sacral space, analogue of the Universe, and what he did was mythologically substantiated by the divine order put down in Chapter I of the treatise and considered given by Brahmā.

* * *

The next part of the rite was divided from the previous by considerable time, starting at sunset, and again consecrated the stage—the holy of holies. In the beginning, a ritual space was arranged and a model of the Universe made on stage. The *maṇḍala* once again assumed its world-forming function, only this time it was not symbolical, as in the *Pūrvaraṅga*, but visible, drawn on the stage by the *Ācārya*, who precisely arranged the ritual site in space by orienting it on the four sacral directions and dividing in eight sectors according to the four cardinal and four intermediate points—a re-creation of cosmic harmony, which the stage repeated.

The centre was brought out next, and occupied by Brahmā as in the *Pūrvaraṅga*, with Śiva and Viṣṇu in the east—the holiest point, and the *Lokapāla*s guarding their points. The rest of the gods, both from the higher and lower hierarchical levels, were within the *maṇḍala,* each in his particular sector. The abode of all gods at once, the stage was the Holy of Holies, a likeness of the sacrificial altar, and the site of another *pūjā*—the basic sacrament in *Nāṭyaśāstra* rites.

As we can assume from the treatise, this part of the consecration demanded the longest *pūjā,* whose description is extremely detailed. Here, the gods were worshipped not only with water, incense and flower garlands as in the *Pūrvaraṅga,* but with canonical food sacrifices. Each god demanded a particular dish, which gave the offering an amazing variety. The *pūjā* started with worship of the three supreme gods to the sounds of mantras which enumerated their virtues and exploits according to the Hindu heavenly hierarchy, thus confirming the inviolable order of the pantheon, basis of the Universal harmony.

After the worship of and generous sacrifices to all gods, the *Ācārya* started a special liturgy to sanctify the stage, typologically close to altar consecration as in many religions. This interpretation of the given part of theatre consecration is borne out by the religious idea of the house of prayer as a theatre, which goes together with the treatment of the stage as the altar.

* * *

The third, last part of the ceremony, with no direct relation to the theatre consecration, was the first rite performed in the templar space, which by this time had acquired complete sacrality. It started with a new stage arrangement, with a jar, *kumbha* in the centre, and a *jarjara* brought. In keeping with the *Nāṭyaśāstra* ritual canon, the priest next served a *pūjā* for all gods, musical instruments and the *jarjara.* According to the treatise, flower sacrifice to this latter had another essential goal—the consecration of this divine weapon by tying it with multicoloured fabrics to mark the abodes of Brahmā, Śiva, Viṣṇu, *Skanda* and the *Nāgas*, to the sounds of a mantra invoking them to their appointed places. The *Ācārya* again alluded to the legend of the theatre origin, which mentioned that, when he appointed the missions of all deïties, Brahmā pointed out their arrangement in the *jarjara* (*NŚ*.1.91-93). From the symbolic banner of Indra alone, the priestly performance made it many gods' abode. Thus, the rite changed its ritual status, the function of divine weapon, which had saved the first drama, receded into the background as the building fully acquired the protective function. Consecration made the *jarjara* not so much Indra's weapon as an analogue of the *arbor mundi*, with the top in the highest spheres and roots reaching the underworld—the status it had in the *Pūrvaraṅga*.

Its further progress allows us to place the ceremony among royal rites. As far as we can judge, the ceremony in which the King directly participated was of crucial importance for the whole country. Prayers for his victories and his subjects' well-being were not enough—the ruler was to be directly involved in the sacral sphere, attending the temple in the new and freshly consecrated building whose holy atmosphere increased his clan.

Surrounded by dancers[39] made-up as goddesses and personifying them, the King entered the sacral scenic space. The *Nāṭyaśāstra* makes it easy to reconstrue these goddesses' names. Most probably, these were the seven *Nāṭya* mothers enumerated in the *Ācārya*'s prayer. Of tremendous interest is the merger of the missions of this rite—heavenly protection of the *Nāṭya* and prosperity bestowed on the King. The divine patronesses of the drama at the same time protect the sovereign, safeguard his life and make it easier for him to penetrate the world of the gods. Femininity and royalty blended in one—a mystical union of the principal carriers of the sacral energy; the two who stood closer to the suprapersonal world than any other community member. The solemn esotericism of the rite created the sensation of actual divine presence on stage, with flames, water sprinkling and prayers all meant a kind of deification of the King and sacralisation of his rule.

Further on, the rite was, doubtless, meant to increase his sacral potential as the ruler on top of the social and clerical hierarchies. To grant him victory, the *Ācārya* broke a *kumbha* and ran round the holy space with a lamp, which he later placed on the stage to symbolize the King's conquest of the world. The fight, with its bloody injuries, forecast the enemy's inescapable doom and the country's affluence.

* * *

As we can easily notice, the ceremonies of the foundation,

building and consecration of the theatre belong to the class of *pūjā*, a type of sacrifice which we know from the *Pūrvaraṅga*, varied in all the *Nāṭyaśāstra* rituals. They had more common features than differences, which were few and minor. The *Pūrvaraṅga* had more music and pageantry, whereas the rites of theatre foundation and consecration were, to all appearances, meant for small congregations, and so were more austere and esoteric. With different ritual goals, all *Nāṭyaśāstra* ceremonies demonstrated one and the same type of religious mentality, sharing ritual semantics, liturgical structure, arrangement of the sacrificial site, ritual symbolism and the manner of offering—in short, all components of which consists the conceptual basis of religious mentality. Symptomatically, the treatise describes an all-embracing ritual complex concerning many aspects of religious life, rather than random rites. It is an essential task to discern the place of the *Nāṭyaśāstra* rites in ancient Indian ritual culture and see whether they belonged to the scenic sacral practice proper, which rose and evolved only as connected with the dramatic performances, or were part of a more comprehensive system of ritual views.

THE SCENIC RITES IN THE *YAJÑA* CONTEXT

F.B.J. Kuiper was the only one to propose a solution to this problem. His concept regards the *Nāṭyaśāstra* rites as part and parcel of Vedic ritualism—an equivalent of *yajña*, the Vedic offering[40]. This view of the *Nāṭyaśāstra* rites stems from the following words in the treatise: "*Yajñena saṃmitaṁ hy etad raṅgadaivatapūjanaṁ*" (This *pūjā* for the deities of the stage is similar to the *yajña*—*NŚ*.1.126; 3.96). However, this premise, twice met in the text, looks more like a comparison of two different rites than their identification with each other. More than that, the *Nāṭyaśāstra* never uses the term *yajña* for more detailed descriptions of scenic rites but always uses the word *pūjā*. This alone makes us doubt the assumption that scenic rites took shape within the *yajña* system. To take a closer view of the matter, we shall compare Vedic worship, with its detailed description in the Brāhmaṇa texts, with the *pūjā* sacrifice described in the *Nāṭyaśāstra*. Ramified and multi-structured, the Vedic cult ideas make us start with a characteristic of the ritual archetype as the basis of rites in the *yajña* circle.

The special and most reliable sources on priestly practices—*Brāhmaṇas* and *Sūtras*—offer diverse approaches to the classification of Vedic rites proceeding from the number of priests involved, time and length of performance, etc. One description bases on ritual functions and singles out the pattern they share. It allows to divide all *yajña* rites in three basic types, with seven particular forms in each: the *Somayajña*, *soma* libation; the *Haviryajña*, fire sacrifice of milk, clarified melted butter and grain; and the *Pākayajña*, home worship better known as the *Gṛhya* (GopBr.1.5.25).

The *Brāhmaṇas* also record a hierarchy of these three types of worship. *Somayajña*, the crucial rite, could be performed only by the twice-born, Brahmins, and demanded high professionalism. The *Haviryajña* came next. The simplest worship, *Pākayajña*, stood the lowest and was every day performed by the head of a household.

The *Nāṭyaśāstra* rites are evidently ceremonial and official, rather than domestic. So their comparison with the Vedic *Somayajña* and *Haviryajña* seems natural. We needn't compare them to the numerous particular types of worship, as all *Soma* offerings ascend to the common ritual pattern of *Agniṣṭoma*, whereas *Haviryajña* rites were based on simple fire sacrifices. They now received an independent ritual function, now were parts of the *Agniṣṭoma*. So we need merely to compare the *pūjā* structure, as singled out in our study of the *Nāṭyaśāstra* rites, with the *Agniṣṭoma* ritual pattern—the most detailed and universal kind of Vedic worship—to say whether the scenic ritual was part and parcel of Vedic ritual culture.[41]

As shown above, all *Nāṭyaśāstra* rites started with the establishment of a ritual space. Vedic rites of the *Agniṣṭoma* type reached the purpose by mounting the altar, the holiest of all structures and the site of the rite proper. The altar accounted for the principal mission of ritual space sacralisation and represented the globe in the Vedic offering.

The *Nāṭyaśāstra* rites arranged the cult space in a totally different way, the *maṇḍala* taking the place of the absent altar. The symbolism of a circle with the centre emphasised and a vertical axis, perhaps, belongs to the world's oldest cult ideas, and is found in many cultures totally unrelated with each other. Nevertheless, the *maṇḍala* as a magic circle was never known in Vedic ritualism. We never come across its description in ritual texts of the Vedic era, connected with the *yajña* system alone.

Vedic religion was based on fire worship, and recognized only fire sacrifices. The *Agniṣṭoma* gave a preparatory status to Vedic priests' long ritual action which framed the central event—the kindling of altar fire and committing the offering to it. The dualism of fire and offering had an all-embracing significance in Vedic theology to determine the innermost, esoteric fundamentals of religion. Identified with *Agni*, fire had exceptional ritual functions as intermediary between the heavenly and mortal worlds. In the non-canonical Vedic worship, gods were ideal presences at the altar, so only the unseen offering, consumed by *Agni* could reach them to give them satisfaction and satiety. In the *Pākayajña* and *Haviryajña*, milk and melted butter was poured onto the fire, and grain thrown in it. *Somayajña* added to them sacrificial animals dismembered on one of the altars. However, it was *soma*, the basic ritual libation of the Vedic era, that embodied the universal offering. Herb gathering, the squeezing and diluting of its juice, and pouring it on the fire were the most secret and sacral instances of the *Agniṣṭoma* type of worship.

As we can easily notice, the *Nāṭyaśāstra* rites imply offerings of an entirely different kind. Fire is neither the only nor even the basic way of sacrifice. The ritual offerings of flowers, incense, unguents, food and water don't need it as an intermediary, with sacrifices piled at the foot of a ritual symbol. Animal sacrifices are absent, and there are no references to *soma*, whereas the *Agniṣṭoma* rites revolved round manipulations with it.

The different types of sacrifice account for the difference in ritual symbolism. Vedic rites never offered flowers, and garlands—more decorative than sacral—were met in the *yajña* rites only on rare occasions. On the whole, the *pūjā* sacrifice has more aestheticism and a simpler form than over-complicated fire magics of the Vedic sacrifice.

Another basic distinction between *yajña* and the *Nāṭyaśāstra* rites is connected with the goals and results of the offering. The Vedic rite was always ordered by a particular donor, who often took part in it, on his own or with his wife, as the case might be. The rite served his well-being, and all the fruit of an auspicious sacrifice belonged to him alone—the person who paid for the ceremony and distributed the *dakṣiṇā* among the priests. The *Nāṭyaśāstra* rites had no such personal address. Though the treatise repeatedly alludes to the patron of the theatre *(Prekṣākartṛ, Prekṣāpati, Arthapati* and *Śabhāpati)*—possibly, also its sponsor—it never points out that the scenic rites should be performed for him alone. Instead, as the treatise says on several occasions, the rites served the prosperity of the country and nation, i.e., had a pronounced communal message.

We can thus state that not one of the essential aspects of religious practice, which determined the arrangement of the ritual space, the way of offering sacrifices and the ritual goals of the worship, offered a coincidence between the Vedic system and the *Nāṭyaśāstra* rites. The comparison allows us to say with certainty that *yajña* and *pūjā* represented archetypes differing in the sacrificial structure, symbolism and theological background. In fact, the Vedic and the *Nāṭyaśāstra* rites served different gods, and actualized different sacral ideas. As we see it, *yajña* could not evolve into *pūjā* through any transformation, without shattering the pivots of Vedic ritualism. We could suppose equal coexistence of *yajña* and *pūjā* within Vedic culture, if not for the conspicuous absence of *pūjā* in all ritual sources of the Vedic era. In other words, this type of adoration was absent in the Vedic ritual system.

Probably, this is the context within which to interpret the *Nāṭyaśāstra* quotation on which F.B.J. Kuiper based his hypothesis and which was the starting point for our comparison of Vedic and scenic rites. The compiler of the treatise must have been well aware of the *yajña-pūjā* difference, and his comparison merely emphasised the elevated status of *pūjā* sacrifice, with sacral results no lesser than *yajña*. To all appearances, scenic rites can be considered similar to Vedic in this sense only.

As we argue that *pūjā* belonged to a thoroughly different type of rite than *yajña*—not merely was non-equivalent to it—we, however, can't but notice the similarity of their numerous components. Thus, the description of the scenic adoration of gods includes a rite which allows Vedic parallels—*Homa*, part of the royal rite which crowned the theatre consecration ceremony. However concise its description (merely mentioning that a *Homa* shall be performed by pouring butter into the fire) it makes the Vedic nature of this rite evident. In all respects, *Homa* coincides with analogous rites widespread in the Vedic era and belonging to the *Haviryajña* as its varieties. However, it held a modest place in the *Nāṭyaśāstra* rites, as an interpolation of a kind in a totally different sacrifice, whereas Vedic rites made fire sacrifice the one and only way of ritual offering.

Doubtless, there is also an affinity between the *jarjara* and the *yūpa*, Vedic sacrificial pillar erected in the ceremonial rites. They looked exactly alike—long wooden poles made in a special way [42]—and had analogous ritual functions. On the one hand, both had a protective mission, and on the other, embodied the vertical axis of the ritual space as *arbor mundi* symbols. The *yūpa* was mainly used in the *Agniṣṭoma* rites. The Vedic priest brought it to the ritual site, sprinkled it with water and erected it, saying a mantra which called it to protect the three worlds—the firmament, the air and the earth, symbolically identified with its three parts (*ŚBr*.III.7.1.4-10). The erection of the *jarjara* involved similar ritual actions as an analogous request was addressed to it—to grant well-being to the earthly world and safeguard the drama. These similarities make us see the *yūpa* and the *jarjara* as one and the same ritual symbol common to the *Nāṭyaśāstra* and Vedic rites. They shared not only the cult mission but the ritual semantics—a factor which disperses all doubts on this score. Brāhmaṇas theology saw the *yūpa* as incarnating the *vajra*, Indra's mace (*ŚBr*.III.7.2.1). The *Nāṭyaśāstra* similarly interprets the *jarjara*—as "incarnation of the *vajra*, the *Daityas*' bane" (*NŚ*.1.91). This untrivial interpretation of a sacrificial pillar could hardly come to the scenic ritualistic system without Vedic influences.

However, the sacral pillar of the *pūjā* had individual features unknown in Vedic ritualism—the name of *jarjara*, rooted in the legend of the drama genesis, and, significantly, a different ritual status. Vedic rites knew no *yūpa* worship, while the *Nāṭyaśāstra* cites the *jarjara* among the three established receivers of *pūjā* sacrifice.

Other, minor details of Vedic and the *Nāṭyaśāstra* rites also offer typological similarities. In both, priests prepared for the rite with fasting, ablutions and wearing new unwashed raiments (*ŚBr*.III.1.2.2-20; *NŚ*.3.3). A number of ritual procedures are also analogous—the ritual space, objects and sacrificers purified and consecrated by sprinkling, and the reading of mantras, to name but two. Many ritual foods which the *Nāṭyaśāstra* points out for scenic worship were known as such back in the Vedic era—refined melted butter, *Madhuparka*, *Pāyasa* and others. The performance of rites at sacral time—a season or an auspicious month and part of day—specified by the celestial position of *Nakṣatra*, particular stars, was also inherited from the Vedic era.

As these similarities between particular varieties of *yajña* and *pūjā* show, scenic rites took shape not in isolation from Vedic ritual culture but inherited its numerous elements. The major differences we pointed out above are more telling, however. Details shared by Vedic adoration and the *Nāṭyaśāstra* rites do not refute our general conclusion that judging by its principal characteristics, the scenic ritual complex was no part of Vedic ritualism but belonged to a different system of religious beliefs and another ritual archetype.

THE SCENIC RITES IN THE *PŪJĀ* CONTEXT

This conclusion makes us go on with our search for analogies of the *Nāṭyaśāstra* ritual complex. Apart from the *yajña* system, topical in the Vedic era, the Indian tradition knew only one all-embracing religious system with a ramified cult practice—we mean the culture which called itself *Ārya Dharma*, better known today as Hinduism[43]. Its worship of gods was based on a rite which shared the name of the *Nāṭyaśāstra* rites—*pūjā*. All *Āgamas*, Hindu ritual texts, irrespective of confession (Śaivate, Viṣṇuite and Kṛṣṇaite) describe one type of sacrifice, with variants within the single *pūjā* ritual pattern[44]. *Āgamic* texts are little studied and were for a long time regarded as sectarian writings at odds with the canonical tradition. In reality, however, their role in the Hindu system repeated that of *Brāhmaṇas* in the Vedic time, as the latest studies show [45].

By comparing *yajña* and *pūjā*, we set side by side the arrangement of the ritual space, the manner of sacrifice and the ritual goals of adoration. Let us retain this order as we compare the *Nāṭyaśāstra* rites with Hindu types of worship as described in the *Śaiva Āgamas* [46].

The *Nāṭyaśāstra* and *Āgamic* rites similarly arranged the sacrificial space—with the *maṇḍala* oriented on cardinal points. As pointed out above, scenic ritualism demanded the magic circle made during the rites. *Āgamic* texts also refer to permanent *maṇḍala*s in places of worship (*Raur.*19.1-7; *Mṛg.*8.52), which structurally repeated the scenic *maṇḍala*. The *Āgamic maṇḍala* had the most sacral point in the centre, where flowers were spread during the rituals, and *kumbha*s placed—essential ritual symbols of Hindu deities (*Aj.*27.39-53; 64-90; 120-129). Special among the jars of various shapes and sizes was the *Śiva-kumbha*, ritual embodiment of Śiva, always placed in the centre of the principal *maṇḍala*. Thus, *Āgamic* rites were analogous to the *Nāṭyaśāstra* as the centre of the sacral space protected by the supreme god—Śiva, in this particular confessional tradition. The circle of the *Āgamic maṇḍala*—visible border of the particular sacrificial space and at the same time of cosmos—was guarded by the *Lokapāla*s, as in the *Nāṭyaśāstra* rites, who took their places to the four cardinal points (*Mṛg.*3.22-23).

Hindu rites had a vertical axis, *dhvaja*, Śiva's banner. According to *Āgamic* theology, the god was present in it during worship, just as Brahmā, Śiva, Viṣṇu, *Skanda* and the *Nāga*s were present in the *jarjara* during scenic rites. All crucial moments of the *Āgamic dhvaja* worship have direct parallels in the description of *jarjara* adoration (*Aj.*27.28-174; *Raur.*18.68-69; 110-148). The divine banner was decorated for the *Āgamic* sacrifice, and erected on its site. Like the *jarjara*, it was the pivotal object of the *pūjā*.

The *Nāṭyaśāstra* and *Āgamic* texts evidently reveal one concept of the ritual space, sharing not only formal arrangement but sacral semantics. Both in *Āgamic* and scenic rites, the centre of the *maṇḍala* represents the centre of the Universe, its circle the world border-line, and the banner the cosmic axis and *arbor mundi*. This makes the arranged ritual space a miniature replica of the whole and organized Universe. Thus, whatever takes place in it has a Universal impact.

Āgamic texts name *pūjā* as the basic ceremonial rite, and present its content and details exactly like the *Nāṭyaśāstra* worship. The *Āgamic* rituals were also performed with flowers, fruit, incense, water and foods in honour of gods and basic ritual symbols (*Aj*.27.112-150; *Mṛg*.3.29-32; 4.107). The *Āgamic pūjā*, with its worship of a god's image or symbol, was not fully unified in the structural aspect in the various Hindu confessions. With the common archetype retained, names of certain ritual actions and their sequence were at variance. The *Śaiva pūjā*, in its most detailed version, traditionally comprised 16 obligatory stages[47] comparable to the basic parts of the *Nāṭyaśāstra* sacrifice.

The *Āgamic pūjā* was preceded by bells and shells, whose sound announced the starting of worship and put the congregation into a praying mood. This overture was followed by the *Ācārya* entering the ritual space with invocation of a god—or several gods—to the site. This sacrament, which demanded an *Āvāhana*, with the god's name repeatedly called, was usually accompanied by music of the same bells and shells. The *Nāṭyācārya* did a similar performance as he addressed his prayers to Hindu gods at the start of theatre consecration.

In the *Āgamic pūjā*, the god to whom the worship was directly addressed was greeted next (*Svāgata*). Then came prayers expressing the congregation's adoration (*Praṇāma*). The image or symbol of this god was decorated with garlands, after which a prayer was addressed to him with an invocation to take the place intended for him (*Āsana*). A statue of the god or the elevation on which his symbol was placed was the next object of worship. After this, the worshipped god was considered present in the ritual space. The congregation saw him in his anthropomorphous image or symbol—most often, a *kumbha* with water. The likeness of these ritual stages to what the *Ācārya* did to consecrate a theatre is evident.

The next part of the Śaiva sacrifice demanded water brought to the site to wash the god's feet or the elevation on which his ritual symbol stood (*Pādya*). Water sprinkling was followed by the *Ācamana*, twice performed by the *Ācārya*, rinsing his mouth with water taken in small gulps out of palms cupped together. Similarly, the *Nāṭyaśāstra* rites included water sprinkling and ablutions before the *Ācamana*, performed by the *Sūtradhāra* in the *Pūrvaraṅga* and the *Ācārya* in the rite of the theatre consecration.

After the *Ācamana*, the Śaiva priest recited mantras as he solemnly circled the god's image or the elevation bearing his symbol (*Pradakṣinā*)—similar to the one performed by the *Sūtradhāra* in the third *Parivarta* as he made a round of the cult space with Brahmā in the centre.

The next part of the *Āgamic pūjā* revolved round the distribution of sacrificial gifts (*Balidāna*). *Bali*, the *Āgamic* name of the offering, is also met in the *Nāṭyaśāstra*, in whose rites it was a crucial stage in the scenic sacrament—a ritual form unknown in the Vedic times but widespread in Hinduism. The *Nāṭyaśāstra* relates *Bali* offerings to gods to the birth of the *Nāṭya* and the construction of the first theatre, when Brahmā, while setting *pūjā* rules, pointed out the *Bali* as part of scenic sacrifice (NŚ.1.123-124). By *Bali*, Hindus meant many kinds of ritual offerings, which we can conventionally subdivide into three groups, which we know from the *Nāṭyaśāstra* descriptions. It could consist of flowers, incense, unguents and water, as in many *pūjā* forms; of ritual foods—*Madhuparka*, boiled rice, honey, milk, melted butter and various kinds of ricemeal with milk; or grain, mustard and saffron seed, sandal paste and ointments.

The *Ācārya* made the offering and put flowers (*Puṣpa*) at the foot of the statue or ritual pedestal and water, perfumed and coloured (*Gandha*) and pure (*Arghya*), next burning incense (*Dhūpa*) to start the ceremony in which the *Dīpa*, burning lamp, was placed in the ritual space—an act of crucial import. When a lamp was brought and brightly lit the entire space, the *Āgamic* tradition saw it as the spreading of grace and consolidation of the divine element, which ousted demonic darkness before the congregation's eyes—a rite analogous to lighting the theatre with the burning *Dīpa*, lamp.

The lamp was always placed to the left of the holy image, the spot on which fruit and all foods which did not demand fire cooking were displayed at the next *pūjā* stage, the food offering (*Prasāda* or *Naivedya*). Cereals and other boiled food was placed on the right. This ritual action was usually accompanied with mantra recitations. This part of the *Āgamic pūjā* has a direct analogue in the food offerings to the gods the *Ācārya* had placed on stage in the middle of the theatre consecration rite. Coincident are the cult idea of worship by food sacrifice, the offerings themselves and the accompaniment with laudatory mantras.

In the *Prārthanā* prayer which ended the *Śaiva pūjā*, the god was asked for the congregation's well-being—analogous to repeated *Nāṭyaśāstra* prayers, which also sought divine mercy and protection, whose earnest a successful rite was.

Both *Āgamas* and the *Nāṭyaśāstra* demanded flowers spread on the site throughout the ceremony. This was an essential component of *pūjā* sacrifice. In the *Nāṭyaśāstra* rites, the fourth priest threw flowers all about the stage at the *Pūrvaraṅga* start, while the *Sūtradhāra* spread them in the centre of the scenic *maṇḍala* as he worshipped Brahmā. In the *Āgamic pūjā*, flowers were spread before the image or symbol of Śiva in worship of the supreme god, like in the *Nāṭyaśāstra*. During *pūjā* to Śiva, "[the *Ācārya*], who knoweth faith, shall turn [his disciple] face toward [Śiva], [and] full of piety, put worshipped flowers into the palms [of the disciple, held in the gesture of] *añjali*, and then shall make [him] throw [them] before [Śiva]" (*Mṛg*.7.59). In *Dikṣā*, *Āgamic* initiation, the novice also threw flowers on the *kumbha*, believed to be the abode of Śiva, placed in the centre of the ritual space. Flower spreading was the most solemn instance of the rite. Apart from the novice's worship, it had another ritual function—the novice received a new, sacral name depending on whether the flowers fell on top of the vessel or toward one of the cardinal points (*Mṛg*.8.60-63).

As we study the ritual goals of the *Āgamic* worship, we must point out that, like the *Nāṭyaśāstra* rites, it had a communal message and was meant not for a particular donor but for the affluence of the whole community. The communal idea was intrinsic in Hindu ritualism. The entire congregation directly participated in the liturgy, the priest made sacrifices on its behalf, and success of the rite guaranteed protection and well-being for each of its members. As the *pūjā* made him closer to the divine world, every believer could address his prayer to god with his personal entreaty, whereas the Vedic religion gave this right only to the person who ordered the offering, and sometimes his family.

* * *

As this comparison reveals, the basic, archetypal aspects of the *Āgamic pūjā* coincided with rites described in the *Nāṭyaśāstra*. The closeness of symbols and worship structure hints at direct genetic links—not mere typological likeness—between the *Nāṭyaśāstra* and *Āgamic* rites. This is borne out by numerous particular analogies, as connected with liturgical practices.

The *Āgamic* rites attached special import to *Nyāsa* postures and *Mudrā* gestures, as demonstrated throughout the worship[48]. Both closely corresponded to canonical features of the anthropomorphous god. As was believed, by demonstrating these gestures and attitudes participants of the rite abstracted from their earthly self as they received *Śakti*, sacral elan, and rose to a divine essence. *Āgamic* theology treated attitudes and gestures as specific forms of communion with gods, which allowed mystically to be transformed into them. Symbolically significant poses and conventional gestures were unlike natural ones and considered iconic manifestations of the divine element. *Āgamic* treatises usually devoted a special chapter to the descriptions of *Nyāsas* and *Mudrās* (*Aj*.26.1-66; *Mṛg*.5.1-18).

As we showed in the analysis of scenic rites, analogous gestures and postures were important in the *Nāṭyaśāstra* ceremonies. They were also used in dramas proper as an expressive means of the ancient Indian theatre. The treatise gives them a detailed description as *Āṅgika abhinaya*, a particular kind of scenic representation. Gestures enabled dramatic performers to demonstrate their characters' emotional state and communicate versatile information connected with the plot without words. Importantly, the conventional idiom of attitudes and gestures used in the rites was closely linked with the formation of the theatrical tradition. It originated with the drama and was developed upon throughout centuries together with other expressive means of acting. Attitudes were the basis of scenic movement and dancing, and gestures conveyed numerous images and categories.

The *Nāṭyaśāstra* devotes two chapters to scenic movement. Chapter XI analyses *Cārī* movements and XII, *Maṇḍala*. We shall not go into detail on particular varieties of movement but merely point out that half the possible stage movements served to enact divine characters of the *Nāṭya*. A system of tricks was elaborated to create the impression of airy grace characteristic of gods, not endowed with solid, heavy flesh. Here, it is apt to remind that the *Nāṭyaśāstra* description of the *Pūrvaraṅga* repeatedly stresses the grace and ease of the *Sūtradhāra*'s movement as he performed divine steps of the *Sūcī* and *Atikrānta Cārī* types.

Apart from particular varieties of movement, Chapter XI describes the six basic *Sthāna* attitudes, many of which the *Sūtradhāra* assumed in the *Pūrvaraṅga*. Each of them corresponded to a deity—which is most important. Thus, the *Samapāda* was associated with Brahmā; *Alidha*, Śiva; *Vaiṣṇava*, Viṣṇu; *Vaiśakha*, Skanda, and *Maṇḍala*, Indra (NŚ.11.51-72).

Many analogues of the *Āgamic* ritual attitudes are offered by dance movements described in the *Nāṭyaśāstra*, Chapter IV. We can't but notice that many of them were closely linked with cult practices. Some, like the *Sthānas* of Chapter XI, were associated with particular gods—*Āvṛtta*, or *Āvarta*, with *Kubera*, *Skhalita* the King of the *Nāgas*, and *Viṣṇukrānta* Viṣṇu. Many demonstrated Śiva in his numerous hypostases—*Talasaṃsphoṭita*, the good god, source of mercy and protection, and *Añcita*, *Bhujangatrāsita* and others, Naṭarāja, King of dance, to name but two. *Niśumbhita* fixed an extremely sophisticated movement, which signified the central moment of Universal destruction in the *Tāṇḍava* orgiastic dance[49].

Many dramatic postures fixed, in a way, the actions of *pūjā* performers. *Vakṣaḥsvastika* and *Pṛṣṭhesvastika* were special for prayer and meditation. *Atikrānta*, in the floral symbolism, portrayed flowers and garlands. *Talapuṣpapuṭa* and *Pārśvanikuṭṭana* signified flower spreading, and *Elakakṛdita* flower offering to a god. To all appearances, a ritual context gave rise to *Daṇḍapada*, symbolising the ritual offering of water, and *Maṇḍalasvastika*, the *maṇḍala* circle.

The *Nāṭyaśāstra* devotes Chapter IX to the gesture language, an essential part of *Āṅgika abhinaya*. It describes 24 gestures with one hand (*Asaṃyuta hasta*), 13 with two simultaneously (*Saṃyuta hasta*) and 30 hand postures in dancing (*Nṛtta hasta*). As follows from detailed precepts of the treatise, manual gestures were hieroglyphic symbols of a rich and peculiar wordless idiom. Finger combinations allowed the actor to express the basic messages of human communication with hardly less precision and detail than in words. As gestures joined in sequences—like words in sentences—he made big monologues based on iconic associations.

Thus, the gestures described in the *Nāṭyaśāstra* are polysemantic and convey the most diverse symbolic categories. Their semantics are largely connected with ritualistic concepts and, doubtless, arose in ritual contexts. Gestures stand for cult actions, symbolizing sprinkling, flower spreading, *Ācamana* and bringing the lamp. *Padmakośa*, the gesture signifying a lotus bud, at the same time symbolized *pūjā* worship (*NŚ*.9.70-72). Gestures also represented gods. *Sūcīmukha*, with the hand going down, stood for Śiva, and a similar gesture with the hand raised to the forehead and crossing it horizontally, for Indra (*NŚ*.9.77-79).

The use of the same gestures and postures in scenic rites and drama performances demands an explanation. As we see it, this explanation lies in the fact that the scenic *pūjā* and the *Nāṭya* were for a long time parts of a single ceremony. Naturally, joint ritual and ritualistic drama performances helped to make discoveries in the field of movement not only to become the basis of an *abhinaya* in the ancient Indian theatre but to enrich the symbolic imagery of the scenic *pūjā*. It is much harder to explain the appearance of analogous gestures and postures in the *Āgamic pūjā* rites which, at first sight, seem unconnected with the evolution of the ancient Indian theatrical tradition. We shall not dwell on this important problem but merely notice that the movement forms of worship we have described may be viewed as proof of common origins of the *Nāṭyaśāstra* and *Āgamic* rites.

Another trait that brought together the *Āgamic* and scenic worship was obligatory musical accompaniment with instruments, ritual singing and dancing. This latter stood out in the structures of many Hindu rites. Some *pūjā* forms finished with pure dance (*Śuddha Nṛtta*), also part of ceremonial worship during *Utsava* festivals (*Raur*.19.1-2). Many *Āgamic* texts have special chapters on cult dancing which, however, specify only ritual actions preceding the *Nṛtta*. Let us analyse a typical description of a ritual dance in the *Rauravāgama* (*Raur*.19.1-8).

The dance was to be performed by a *gāṇika*—young, chaste, beautiful, serene in her spirit and devoid of mercantile interests. She made two ablutions, put on lovely raiments and jewellery, crowned her head with white flowers, washed her feet, and then entered the ritual hall, *Maṇḍapa*, to draw the *maṇḍala* in the stage centre. She sprinkled it with water as she recited incantations, and spread flowers in it, thus worshipping Śiva *Naṭeśvara*, Lord of Dance. Then she sprinkled with water the priestess who assisted her, standing outside the *maṇḍala*, and took flower bunches from her again to spread them in the magic circle, this time in worship of Śiva *Parameśvara*, Supreme God. Then she pressed her palms in the *añjali* gesture and made the *Mudrā* lotus to start dancing to the sound of many instruments, mainly percussion, and ten sacred tunes. The *Rauravāgama* description of the dance finished on this. The end of the chapter contained only a traditional notice of the pivotal sacral role of *Nṛtta* as atoning sins.

It is easy to see that the *Āgamic* ceremony before the dance was analogous to the one of the dancing girl in the *Pūrvaraṅga*. The *Raurava* and other *Āgamas* do not provide concrete characteristics of *Nṛtta*. The texts explain this absence by Bharata's detailed description of dance. In other words, it was described in the *Nāṭyaśāstra* (*Raur*.19.7)—a notable allusion and clear indication that the Hindu religious tradition saw the *Nāṭyaśāstra* chapters on dancing as ritual texts. It was no use to repeat them in *Āgamas*, as the treatise was always at hand. More than that, this *Āgamic* indication makes us revise the customary attitudes to these parts of the *Nāṭyaśāstra* as describing secular, rather than ritual dancing proper. Evidently, not only sections on the scenic *pūjā* canon should be regarded as ritual texts but, at least, in the main, chapters on *Gāndharva* music, dancing, dance poses, and gesticular symbols and techniques.

Worship with postures, gestures, songs, music and dancing belongs to features shared by *Āgamic* and scenic rites. At the same time, the Hindu ritual system allows to single out features common to all three worship practices under review—the Vedic sacrifice *yajña*, *Nāṭyaśāstra* rites and the *Āgamic pūjā*.

As we compared the Vedic and the *Nāṭyaśāstra* rites, we stressed the doubtless succession of the scenic *jarjara* to the Vedic *yūpa*. *Āgamic* rites knew another analogous item, the *dhvaja*, banner staff, outwardly synonymous to the *yūpa* and *jarjara*. The *dhvaja-jarjara* connection is self-evident—both represent one sacral symbol, the divine banner staff. In fact, the *jarjara* is a variety of the *dhvaja* as used in scenic worship and owing its name to the first dramatic performance. Not only the semantics but the ritual function of the *jarjara* and *dhvaja* coincide as pivotal objects of *pūjā* sacrifice. The presence of the *dhvaja*, identical to *jarjara*, in *Āgamic* ritualism allows us to trace the *yūpa-jarjara-dhvaja* connection to see the divine banner of the *Āgamic pūjā* another heritage of the Vedic ritualism.

Another major feature uniting the *yajña* and *pūjā* systems, *Homa*, performed in the royal rite of the *Nāṭyaśāstra*, was inherited by the *Āgamic* tradition without essential change. The Vedic *Homa* was prominent in many Hindu rites. *Āgamas* provide numerous descriptions of *Homa* varieties with flaming braziers brought to the sacrificial site. Like in the Vedic era, *ghee*, melted butter, and milk were poured into the consecrated flame, and grain and other food thrown—all this to mantra recitals (Aj.10.38-44; 27.184-198; Mṛg.8.64).

Similar were the stages of priests' preparations for the rite. Both the Vedic and Hindu times demanded that the priest should fast, make ablutions, put on new, never washed garments, and concentrate on the coming ceremony. This was obligatory for the Vedic *Brāhmaṇa*, the *Nāṭyācārya* of the *Nāṭyaśāstra*, and the priest who performed the *Āgamic pūjā*. Perhaps, it was the ritual *yajña* system that gave the *Āgamic* tradition its sacral practice of water sprinkling, mantra recital, blessing, and timing the rite to lucky-starred days.

We can't but notice that all features of Vedic ritualism revealed in the *Nāṭyaśāstra* rites are present in Hindu ones. In fact, this is one more proof of the close link between *Āgamic* and scenic *pūjā*. Once we compare the *Nāṭyaśāstra* and *Āgamic* rites, we have every reason to say that they belonged to one system of ritual mentality, which determined the fundamentals of theology and particular liturgical traits and details. Evidently, scenic and *Agamic* worship based on a shared archetype, which we can conventionally term the *pūjā* archetype. Though borrowing certain features from Vedic ritualism, this archetype thoroughly differed from the *yajña*, as we see from our comparison of *Nāṭyaśāstra* and Vedic rites.

CHAPTER II

THE DRAMA AS STAGE VERSION OF THE MYTH

As stated above, no scholar has traced as yet direct links between the Sanskrit drama and particular rites, though we could precisely state the religious source of the drama on the basis of these links. In the final analysis, it would be our decisive argument in the long debates about secular or religious ritualistic origins of the Indian theatre. As the author of this book sees it, the solution of this problem comes against complications of both general cultural and methodological nature. As they regard rite-drama relations, scholars seek to trace the succession from the ritual structure to that of the drama[50]; they see the drama hero as the changed ritual performer[51]; or try to discern in the dramatic plot the contextual basis of the myth that gave rise to this drama, or its mythological equivalents[52]. Each of these approaches concerns direct transformation of the rite into the drama. Nevertheless, such historical succession would be possible only if the rite, desacralised in its spontaneous evolution, gave rise to its successor, the drama, as it died away. Without ruling out this development in principle, we only point out that, as we see it, the *Nāṭyaśāstra* presents a different concept of the rite-drama relation, according to which their connection is that of mutual conditioning, rather than succession. In other words, the Sanskrit drama did not succeed to the rite. Neither did it originate out of the rite, but evolved parallel to it as part and parcel of the ritual ceremony.

THE MYSTERIAL GENRES

Chapter XX of the treatise is devoted to the ten kinds of the Sanskrit drama (*Daśarūpaka*) and describes one by one the

Nāṭaka, Prakaraṇa, Samavakāra, Īhāmṛga, Ḍima, Vyāyoga, Utsṛṣṭikāṅka, Prahasana, Bhāṇa and *Vīthī*. The extant drama literature represents only three kinds of the *Nāṭya—Nāṭaka, Prakaraṇa* and *Bhāṇa*. Dramas of these genres emerged in the classical era of the Sanskrit theatre, which had made a long way from its origins and, in fact, evolved into a secular art. The other seven kinds of the drama, whose evolution, to all appearances, took place in pre-classical times, have not come down to us in samples of any authenticity, and we owe our idea of them to their descriptions in treatises, above all, the *Nāṭyaśāstra*. Four genres—*Samavakāra, Ḍima, Īhāmṛga* and *Vyāyoga*—present the greatest scholarly interest. The *Nāṭyaśāstra* singles them out in the group of plays to be performed in a harsh, aggressive (*Āviddha*) manner. According to a generally shared conviction, they took shape before other *Nāṭya* varieties, characterized by a gentler (*Sukumāra*) performing style, and are closer to the sources of the theatre. In Chapter XIV, the *Nāṭyaśāstra* seṭ forth the basic characteristics of the *Āviddha* dramas, recurring practically unchanged in Chapter XXXV. According to the treatise, "the play which requires energetic aggressive (*sattvāviddha*) gestures and dance movements (*Aṅgahāras*) to represent cutting, wounding, challenging and piercing, and contains the use of magic and yogic powers, as well as painting and plastering work (*pusta*) and make-up, and [also] has numerous men and few women [characters] and adopts mainly *Sāttvatī* and *Ārabhaṭī Vṛttis* is called *Āviddha*" (*NŚ*.14.56-57). "Production of the *Āviddha* plays should be made through the gods, *Dānavas* and *Rākṣasas* [represented by actors], who are haughty and endowed with courage, vitality and strength" (*NŚ*.14.59).

As follows from these definitions, *Āviddha* dramas had salient mysterial features and, in fact, were battle scenes of gods and demons, notable for the sacral status of dramatic personae and the events portrayed, for supernatural intercession, and predominance of male characters. These mystery plays had a sophisticated imagery, with props amply used, and the performers made up and costumed.

In their total, these features give us a rather comprehensive idea of the *Āviddha* dramas. However, its most essential features were determined by the category of the style (*Vṛtti*)—to be more precise, a blend of two styles, the *Sāttvatī* and the *Ārabhaṭī*. Each deserves to be described on its own because, as we regard particular kinds of the drama, we shall again and again turn to the concept of style as the pivotal definition of the dramatic genre[53].

The *Sāttvatī, Vṛtti* spiritual style is hard to define. The *Nāṭyaśāstra* has this to say about it: "[The style] which is endowed with the quality of *Sattva*, duels of many kinds (*Nyāya*) and [proper] metrical patterns, has exuberance of joy and completely suppresses the emotion of sorrow is called *Sāttvatī Vṛtti*. This *Vṛtti* is also known to consist of representation of words, gestures and of power in the speeches and acts showing the rise of *Sattva*" (*NŚ*.22.38-39). The *Sattva* is the key concept in these *Vṛtti* descriptions, its qualities fully displayed in the spiritual style.

The doctrine of *Sattva*, the inner spiritual energy, is one of the cornerstones of the ancient Indian theory of drama. The *Nāṭyaśāstra* mentions *Sattva* on many occasions, disclosing the essence of this concept in several definitions. Here we cite the most detailed of these: "*Sattva* means originating in the mind (*manas*). It is caused by the concentrated mind. Through mental concentration the *Sattva* is evolved. This nature of the mind involving horripilation, tears, paleness and the like cannot be properly portrayed by one absent-minded. Such is the *Sattva*, essential in the *Nāṭya*, based as it is on imitating the human nature. How can sorrow, which has weeping as its basis, be represented by one who is not sorry? And how can happiness, which has delight as its basis, be represented by one who is not happy? Such is the *Sattva* necessary [for the drama], which is determined by the fact that tears and horripilation should be respectively shown by any performer who is not [actually] sorry or happy"(*NŚ*, p.110).

Thus, by *Sattva* we shall understand a particular concentration of the *manas*. Conventionally translated here as the mind, *manas* is really a more complicated concept, reflecting the body and the mind in their unseverable unity, a merger of the spiritual and the intellectual in man's inner life. In fact, this definition brings out the mechanism by which *Sattva* is aroused, aimed to make the actor perceive the emotions he imitates as strongly and spontaneously as his own through concentration and tension of the *manas*.

As we see it, the *Sattva* doctrine—the basis of the spiritual style—reflects essential features of the ancient Indian concept of the nature of the theatre. Possibly, it stems from a rather early period of drama formation. We have an impression that what is meant here is a unique way of re-creating reality on stage, which demanded of the actor not merely a masterful representation of the outward aspect of his role but full self-identification with the hero—in fact, reincarnation in this hero. Only thus, when the actor brings himself to the necessary mood, can he achieve a mental and emotional state in full keeping with the hero's.

Acting in the spiritual style was, in a sense, the peak of scenic craftsmanship. To all appearances, the ability to live in the part resulted from a system of professional training connected with meditation. This idea comes natural from the *Nāṭyaśāstra* explanations on the *Sāttvatī Vṛtti.* Once he concentrated to overcome sadness and all related emotions, the actor was to nourish limitless joy in himself—an euphoria of a kind—at the same time achieving precision and clarity in this emotional state, for this style "has no place for despondency" (*NŚ*.22.40). Once he accumulated spiritual energy that aroused joy, an ecstasy of strength and a consciousness of might, the actor was to display it in speech and movement full of *Sattva*. There were two ways of scenic representation (*abhinaya*) for this—*Āṅgika,* gesticular action, and *Vācika,* verbal. A third way, *Sāttvika abhinaya,* the performance of the *Sattva,* lay in the very name of the style.

What particularly the actor was supposed to do was specified in the characteristics of the four varieties of the spiritual style. In *Utthāpaka* (lit., Excitement), he encouraged his martial spirit before the performance by saying: "I am getting up [for battle now] and challenging the enemy, 'You can show your strength' " (*NŚ*.22.42). Thus the *Utthāpaka* was a challenge arising from the spirit of rivalry. *Parivartaka* (lit., Consummation) envisaged auxiliary means to increase the martial spirit used whenever necessary. This is the definition for it: "If after living the things which caused the rising up, one adopts other things out of necessity it is called *Parivartaka*" (*NŚ*.22.43).

Saṃlāpaka (lit., Discourse), a third variation of the spiritual style, was a dialogue of opponents who poured abuse at each other before the duel to put fight in themselves. This torrent of abuse sometimes expressed contempt for the enemy (*NŚ*.22.44). The last of the four varieties of the spiritual style, *Saṃghāta* (lit., Fight) principally differed from the three others, practically characterizing a situation in which the use of the *Sāttvatī Vṛtti* was as appropriate as nowhere else. "If for the sake of a friend or some monetary gain or due to a chance occurrence or to [one's] own fault an alliance is disrupted it is called *Saṃghāta*" (*NŚ*.22.45). So an open struggle was inevitable.

As we can judge by the *Nāṭyaśāstra* description, the spiritual style was aimed, above all, for the scenic representation of battles. More than that, it was precisely localized. In *Saṃghāta,* the peaceful course of life was already broken but it was not yet the time for open battle. The enemies only confronted each other and encouraged their martial spirit with the intensity of mind and feeling in *Parivartaka*. Conscious of their strength and the enemy's frailty, having poured derisive abuse at him (*Saṃlāpaka*), the hero challenged him in *Utthāpaka* and started the battle.

Thus, *Sāttvatī Vṛtti* had a direct bearing on the start of a battle. The battle proper was acted out in *Ārabhaṭī Vṛtti,* for which the *Nāṭyaśāstra* had the following description: "The style which includes mostly the qualities of a very bold (*Ārabhaṭa*) persons is known as *Ārabhaṭī*. There is much altercation, deception, bragging and falsehood in it. The style is called *Ārabhaṭī* if there is a representation of modelwork (*pusta*) falling down, jumping, crossing over, deeds of magic and conjuration and different kinds of fighting" (*NŚ*.22.55-56). Descriptions of particular varieties of *Ārabhaṭī Vṛtti* added precision to this basic definition. Thus, *Avapāta* (lit., Fall) "is in those affairs causing fear and jubilation, panic, flurry, many kinds of speaking and quick entrance and exit" (*NŚ*.22.59). *Saṃpheṭa* (lit., Mutual Conflict) represented "all that rises out of excessive excitement and largely involves struggle, duels, deception, split, dissention and clash of weapons" (*NŚ*.22.61). A third variety of *Ārabhaṭī Vṛtti, Vastūtthāpana* (lit., Raising the Plot) "is a brief combination of all *Rasas*, with or without panicky running and sheltering [anyone]" (*NŚ*.22.60).

As we can assume from these definitions, *Ārabhaṭī Vṛtti* was very dynamic and spectacular, with wrestling subtly imitated by particular stunts, lightning motions (*Cārī*) and sophisticated scenic movement (*Karaṇa*). No doubt, it had a great degree of verisimilitude in the audience's eyes. The use of special stage effects was evident to portray magic and the interference of witchcraft. Underhand tricks—deception of the enemy and treachery—added to the overall tension.

This style also had modelworks (*pusta*, as the *Nāṭyaśāstra* termed them) among its expressive means. Chapter XXIII, with its detailed descriptions of scenery, costumes and make-up, mentioned weaponry, shields, banners, stuffed elephants and other animals, vehicles made for the performance, hills and even palatial buildings (*NŚ*.23.8). In keeping with *Nāṭyaśāstra* precepts, the actors smashed these props for the battle scene to have more effect on the audience.

Characteristically, the props not merely added pageantry to the performance but had semantics all their own. In particular, the definition of the fourth variety of *Ārabhaṭī Vṛtti* says: "That which is called *Saṃkṣiptaka* (lit., Constriction), in keeping with the literal meaning of the term, is furnished with relevant craftsmanship. Presentation of the modelworks, drawings and dresses is its main feature. The plot [thus can be] extremely condensed" (*NŚ*.22.58). As we see it, this definition points out that sophisticated props, painted scenery and impressive costumes spoke for themselves and rendered lengthy monologues needless, thus making the performance dynamic as the plot rapidly unfolded. More than that, it is evident that the word, and the related *Vācika abhinaya*, were not in the centre of the forceful style. Of all kinds of stage representation, *Āṅgika abhinaya*, expressive movement, held pride of place; next came *Āhārya abhinaya*, which revealed the content through props, costumes and make-up.

It is easy to see that both these styles had much in common. Their description in the *Nāṭyaśāstra* allows us to reconstrue the common features of the *Āviddha* dramas, with *Sāttvatī* and *Ārabhaṭī Vṛtti*s as obligatory elements. The starting point was in a conflict between gods and demons, with the following encouragement of mutual hatred. The battle scene brought the climax and, to all appearances, took up the better part of the performance. The sumptuous properties, costumes, modelworks and scenery not merely made the acting all the more convincing but carried information as to the place of action, and the characters' position and hierarchical status. The movement, not the word, determined the expressive power of stage battles, in which the gesticular idiom evidently prevailed over the verbal.

SAMAVAKĀRA. THE MYTH OF THE CHURNING OF THE OCEAN

From general characteristics of the *Āviddha* performances, we shall now go over to particular varieties of mystery plays. The *Nāṭyaśāstra* qualified the *Samavakāra* as the oldest of these, tracing the entire dramatic tradition to it. As the legend of the divine origin of *Samavakāra*, which opens Chapter IV (*NŚ*.4.1-14) has it, when Brahmā started the art of drama in times immemorial, he not merely stated the order of the scenic rite but wrote the first play, which he named *Samavakāra* to be premiered before all gods, and later repeated for Śiva.

Chapter XX contains a genre, not mythological description of the *Samavakāra*[54] as a particular form of spectacle with a canonical set of compositional features. According to the *Nāṭyaśāstra*, the *Samavakāra* "shall be composed of events which served as [seed of] discontent between gods and *Asuras*. It [shall be] glorious, sublime and devoid of sadness (*prakhyātodāttanāka*) and comprise three parts [to present] three kinds of deception (*Kapaṭa*), three kinds of excitement (*Vidrava*) and three kinds of love (*Śṛṅgāra*). [Besides, it ought to have] twelve characters and consist of eighteen *Nāḍikās*" (*NŚ*.20.64-65). The treatise fixes the length of every part with "the rule of its parts — the number of the *Nāḍikās* each [should] include and their arrangement" (*NŚ*.20.65). According to it, "the part containing the comic element (*Prahasana*), excitement (*Vidrava*), deception (*Kapaṭa*) and elements of the Vīthī, and limited to twelve *Nāḍikās* shall go first. Then follows the second part containing the same [components] but limited to four *Nāḍikās*. The third part shall contain two *Nāḍikās*, according to precepts on the plot (*Vastu*) length. The composition must take into account that [all parts] shall differ in topic from one another. [More than that,] the topics in the *Samavakāra* are to be closely related to one another (*pratisandhāna*)" (*NŚ*.20.67-69).

Let us first regard formal structural characteristics of the *Samavakāra*. The presence of three practically isolated parts is the main. As the *Nāṭyaśāstra* stresses, each is entitled to a theme all its own, which makes it, in fact, an independent drama. Contemporary scholarly literature treats the *Samavakāra* as a three-act play, though its description in the *Nāṭyaśāstra* hardly gives ground for this interpretation as, from the point of content, the form of multi-act drama presupposes a single plot divided into parts as it evolves, but retains the unity of action throughout the play. The *Samavakāra* breaks this basic rule. As the treatise has it, the genre was intrinsically devoid of an integral plot to be divided into parts and presented as three consecutive episodes. The fact that the play was broken between parts, and a new action started, allows us to see each of the *Samavakāra* parts a play on its own. In this sense, it was rather a trilogy of independent one-act plays united only by being enacted one after another.

The incoherence, semantic and structural isolation of the *Samavakāra* parts turns out the basic feature of this genre, never put to doubt in the later tradition. Almost all medieval authors mentioned it as they commented the treatise or wrote works of their own on the drama (*AbhBh*, vol.II, p.439; *BhPr*, p.249; 1.11-18; *ND*, p.109; *SD*, p.437; *NLRK*. 2816).

Precisely fixed length was another pivotal formal characteristic of the *Samavakāra*. As the *Nāṭyaśāstra* has it, the play consisted of eighteen *Nāḍikās*. According to definition, a *Nāḍikā* is half of the *Muhūrta*, 48 minute period, and so is 24 minutes long. Part One, the longest, with twelve *Nāḍikās*, took about five hours, and Part Two, with four, slightly over an hour and a half, leaving less than an hour to Three, of two *Nāḍikās*. This arrangement allows several observations. First, the wealth of detail in these temporal characteristics reminds of precise descriptions of rites and makes us think that this precision had ritual sources. Second, the precise, rather than approximate indication of time intervals for each act supposes their correlation with three particular plots within the specified intervals, re-enacted in the *Samavakāra* again and again. Evidently, the topics were unequal in importance, with the initial dominating. Five hours of unbroken scenic action to disclose a single theme alone showed the sophistication and exceptional significance of its content. The two stories that followed were much shorter, with the number of events portrayed necessarily reduced.

In Chapter XX, the *Nāṭyaśāstra* does not directly point out the topics to be enacted in *Samavakāra*, but gives their oblique characteristics in ample detail. The basic genre definition says that *Samavakāra* shall present deception (*Kapaṭa*), excitement (*Vidrava*) and love (*Śṛṅgāra*)—three kinds of each—and goes on to explain that each of these plot elements shall in its turn consist of three parts. Thus, "excitement shall be of three kinds: one coming of battle and water (*yuddhajala*); one of the wind, fire and a big elephant (*vāyvagnigajendrasaṃbhrama*), or of the siege of a city (*nagaroparodha*)" (*NŚ*.20.70). "That which is made due to a devised plan (born of the human mind), or [takes place] by chance (by divine will—*devavaśa*), or due to a stratagem of the enemy to give rise to bliss or unhappiness, is three kinds of deception" (*NŚ*.20.71). Last but not least, "love, as prescribed by the Sages and born three ways, shall have three kinds—that which is born by *Dharma* (religious duty), *Kāma* (erotic passion) and *Artha* (material benefit)" (*NŚ*.20.72).

We cannot but notice the emphasized triple structure of the *Samavakāra*. Its three parts included three obligatory elements, in their turn comprising events, causes and effects arranged in threes. These omnipresent triads could hardly come by chance—rather, they incarnated an idea underlying the whole, followed with the utmost consistency. In other words, as we see it, the *Samavakāra* structure was made to purpose and proceeded from the magic of the number "3"—in Indian tradition, the holiest of all and endowed with a unique sacral meaning as reflected in the idea of the triune Universe (*Triloka*), the concepts of the three Vedas, *Trimūrti*, 33 gods of the Hindu pantheon, etc. The number also had an outstanding function in scenic rites—suffice it to mention the three priests who performed the major part of the *Pūrvaraṅga*, the three rounds of the stage by the *Sūtradhāra* in the *Parivartas*, his triple bows and worship of Śiva, Brahmā and Viṣṇu with three steps for the male, female and neuter elements. Doubtless, the triple *Samavakāra* composition also had a profound symbolic and religious message as structural representation of the total, whole and comprehensive content enacted on stage.

One question remains open—the correlation of the three basic plot components in each part of the *Samavakāra*. *Nāṭyaśāstra* definitions give us no precise information on this score. Neither do they offer any oblique indications, leaving us only guesswork. Thus, we can assume that the sequence in which the treatise enumerates the various kinds of *Kapaṭa, Vidrava* and *Śṛṅgāra* corresponded to their arrangement in the three parts of the drama. As we use this formal criterion to arrange them in combinations, we see a plot related to water and a battle in the initial part, in which they created an excitement; there was a prearranged deception, and love based on religious duty. Like-wise, excitement in the next part could be due to the wind, fire and a giant elephant; the deception followed from a train of circumstances, and love was rooted in carnal passion. The final part revolved round a city whose siege bred the suspense; the deception motive was connected with enemy plots, and material interests gave rise to the love.

Some preliminary observations are necessary before we regard the correspondence of these contextual components to the actual content of the *Samavakāra*. First, the definition of *Śṛṅgāra* is the most conventionalized of all triad components. The descriptions of *Dharma Śṛṅgāra, Artha Śṛṅgāra* and *Kāma Śṛṅgāra* look intended more to illustrate the *Trivarga* formula than to characterize an actual plot[55]. This assumption is borne out by the fact that, unlike *Kapaṭa* and *Vidrava, Śṛṅgāra* is never mentioned in the description of the initial part of *Samavakāra*, though detailed enough—it enumerates only laughter, excitement, deception and elements of *Vīthī*. As the second part was based on the same components, according to the *Nāṭyaśāstra*, and nothing is said of the third in this context, we have to assume that *Śṛṅgāra* was absent as plot component at least in the two opening parts. Possibly, it was totally unrelated to them and was mentioned in the *Samavakāra* description only to preserve the symmetrical arrangement which demanded triads.

The definitions of *Kapaṭa*, deception, and *Vidrava*, excitement, were much more concrete—mainly the latter, with its mention of naturalistic details, such as a battle, water, fire, wind, an elephant and a besieged city, to all appearances, borrowed from real life plots re-enacted in each of the three parts. The three kinds of deception, prominent in the dramatic development, also look as adequate enough reflections of a plot borrowed from reality.

Let us leave our conclusions at that and turn for a time from the *Samavakāra* components to other information as to the content of this dramatic genre. According to the *Nāṭyaśāstra*, the plot revolved round events that brewed discord between the gods and the *Asuras*. As it also points out, the staged story was renowned (*prakhyāta*) and sublime (*udātta*)—in other words, was a typical myth of strife between two celestial clans. The god-*Asura* antagonistic pattern remained archetypal in Indian mythology of many eras, and included a passing truce based on balanced forces, an inevitable clash with a battle ensuing, with the gods bound to win. Many myths develop on his pattern. For *Samavakāra*, the *Nāṭyaśāstra* specifies the name with sufficient precision—*Amṛtamanthana* (*NŚ*.4.2)—The Churning of the Ocean, as this myth is known with scholars. Evidently, *Samavakāra* represented a particular myth, as the treatise testifies, however, without citing it. The legend has gone down to us as a long tale in *Ādiparva*, the first Book of *Mahābhārata*[56]. As its content is essential for the drama we are analysing, we shall now proceed to its concise retelling.

In times immemorial, standing high for infinite ages upon Mount Meru once all the mighty celestials sat down and held a conclave. They came in quest of *amṛta*. Seeing the celestial assembly in anxious consultation, Nārāyaṇa said to Brahmā: "Do thou churn the Ocean with the *Suras* (gods) and the *Asuras*. By doing so *amṛta* shall be obtained together with all drugs and all gems. O ye gods, churn ye the Ocean and ye shall discover *amṛta*."

There is a mountain of name Mandara adorned with peaks like those of the clouds. It is the best of mountains and is covered all over with intertwining herbs. The gods took it with them, and came to the Ocean, saying: "O Ocean, we have come to churn thy waters for obtaining nectar." And the Ocean replied: "Be it so, as I am to have a share of the nectar. I am able to bear the agitation of my waters by the mountain." And the gods went to the King of the Tortoises and said to him: "O Tortoise-king, thou shalt have to hold the mountain on thy back." And the Tortoise-king agreed.

And the gods and the *Asura*s made Mandara their churning staff and Vāsuki the cord, and set about churning the main *amṛta*. The *Asura*s held Vāsuki by the hood and the gods by the tail. And in consequence of the friction he received at the hands of the gods and the *Asura*s, black vapours with flames issued out of his mouth which, becoming clouds charged with lightning, poured down showers to refresh the tired gods. And blossoms beginning to rain on all sides of the gods from the trees on the whirling Mandara also refreshed them.

After the churning had gone on for some time the gums of various trees and herbs mixed with the waters of the Ocean. And the celestials attained immortality by drinking the waters mixed with those gums vested with the properties of *amṛta*. By degrees the milky water of the agitated deep produced clarified butter by virtue of the gums and juices. But nectar did not rise even then.

After a while the mild Moon emerged from the Ocean. Thereafter, Lakṣmī dressed in white, and *Surā* the wine goddess, the white steed, and then the celestial gem Kaustubha. Then arose the divine Dhanvantari himself with the white vessel of nectar in his hand. And seeing him the *Asura*s set up a loud cry, saying, "Ye have taken all, he must be ours". Thereupon Nārāyaṇa called his bewitching *māyā* to his aid and assuming a ravishing female form coquetted with the *Asura*s. And the *Daitya*s, ravished with her charms, lost their reason and unanimously placed the nectar in the hands of that fair woman. And then all the tribes of the gods during that time of great fright drank the nectar, receiving from Viṣṇu Nārāyaṇa, quitting his ravishing female form and hurling many terrible weapons at them, made the *Dānava*s tremble. And thus commenced the dreadful battle on the gods and the *Asura*s. And when the battle was raging fiercely, Nara and Nārāyaṇa entered the field. And Nārāyaṇa seeing the heavenly bow in the hand of Nara called to his mind his own weapon—the *Dānava* destroying discus—*Sudarśana*. And *Sudarśana* came from the sky as soon as thought of. And seeing the furious discus scouring the fields of heaven like a blazing flame, the mighty *Dānavas* entered the bowels of the Earth while others plunged into the sea of salt waters.

Assuming that the play corresponded to this legend closely enough, we can compare its plot to the three kinds of excitement, deception and love postulated for the *Samavakāra*. The legend does not mention the besieged city—the centre of the final part of the drama—nor tempests and big elephants, though the water and a battle, the basic components of the initial *Samavakāra* part, are pivotal in the epic myth, with the first part closely connected with the Ocean, and the second with the battle royal between gods and demons. To all appearances, the myth of "The Churning of the Ocean" served as the plot of the initial and principal *Samavakāra* part, five hours long, while the later parts presented other myths, in which we have to make do with oblique characteristics to be found in the *Nāṭyaśāstra*. Like *Amṛtamanthana*, both were, perhaps, linked to the battle mythologeme, though treating of other events, which also made gods clash with demons. We know only that the second plot revolved round an elephant, a tempest and fire, and third round a besieged city. This is not enough to identify the myths with any degree of certainty, and reliable hypotheses require thorough complementary studies. So we limit our analyses to "The Churning of the Ocean"—evidently the principal myth of the *Amṛtamanthana* trilogy—as we trace down the content of the *Samavakāra* and reconstrue its plot.

In correspondence with the mythic development, the action was rather smooth at the start. The gods took their places on the one side of the stage, with the demons on the opposite, and the churning began, with the two groups taking turns in pulling the rope. Hand props were possibly used for the Mandara staff and Vāsuki the Serpent. The stage effects possibly included the sprinkling of the heroes with water and strewing them with flower and leaf garlands, as in the epic myth. The action climaxed when the *amṛta* was ready, and came to a turning point with Viṣṇu Nārāyaṇa's disguise, which caused the great battle. Perhaps, this disguise was the plotted deception.

Next came the scenic battle, whose basic features we can reconstrue from the descriptions of *Sāttvatī* and *Ārabhaṭī Vṛttis*, and the details from *Mahābhārata*. The battle was preluded by the broken pledge as demanded by one *Sāttvatī Vṛtti* variety[57]. To put fight in the gods and intimidate the demons before the battle[58] Viṣṇu "hurling many terrible weapons at them made the *Dānavas* tremble".[59] The characteristic of *Ārabhaṭī Vṛtti* echoes the *Mahābhārata* description of the fierce battle that followed. The stage weapons required by this *Vṛtti* were of great importance in this scene. Thus, Nara had his bow-and-arrows, while Viṣṇu summoned his *Sudarśana* discus by mental effort. Then, "seeing the furious discus scouring the fields of heaven like a blazing flame, the mighty *Dānavas* entered the bowels of the Earth while others plunged into the Sea of salt waters ".[60] This battle scene in *Mahābhārata* reminds of a spectacular stage finale, with the striking effect of a discus descending from heaven. Viṣṇu's weapon can be regarded as a way of plot concision, which the *Nāṭyaśāstra* recommends for *Ārabhaṭī Vṛttī* [61]. The battle could be endless but for the *Sudarśana*, which settled its outcome, rendering the demonic resistance pointless, the long battle is over and the actors who played the *Asuras* left the stage one by one.

The fact deserves a special stress that we reconstrued the *Amṛtamanthana* not merely proceeding from *Mahābhārata* but analysing it as the basis of a scenic play. This interpretation can't be accused of being groundless as justified by the epic structure—a mosaic sequence of episodes. Neither can we rule out direct links and mutual influences of the *Mahābhārata* myth of "The churning of the Ocean", and the *Samavakāra Amṛtamanthana*, which the *Nāṭyaśāstra* calls the first drama. The birth of the *amṛta* myth shall be analysed to specify these links and make more precise the presumed influences.

Mahābhārata presents the *Amṛtamanthana* myth—one of the essential in Hindu mythology—as a detailed and consecutive narration, though the earlier tradition has not yet revealed its precedents. Vedic literature does not mention the cosmogonic act, which divided the primal waters, stated a new order of things and created fabulous treasures. Many hypotheses sought to explain this conspicuous gap, one by G. Dumezil, major student of Indo-European mythology[62], who drew on Scandinavian, Celtic, Greek, Latin and Persian materials to reconstrue the archetypal basis of the myth, which he traced to the archaic rites of spring, widespread among Indo-Europeans. He derived the idea of the elixir of immortality to the sacral drink used at festivals—wine in Greece, and *soma* or *haoma* with Indo-Āryans. In the extremely extensive mythological context used by Dumezil, the *Mahābhārata* myth is a mere example to illustrate global structures. The scholar saw it as old enough to reflect archaic Indo-European ideas, and sought to demonstrate that the conspicuous silence of the Vedas did not prove its comparative novelty, with Vedic sources generally standing aloof to narrative myths. Not that his explanation of its absence sounds convincing enough. At any rate, it does not cancel further search for the source of this particular epic tradition.

The hypothesis at which K. Geldner came in his Ṛgvedic studies was far more concrete[63]. As he points out, the Veda attaches the idea of *amṛta* to *Soma* and *Havis*, sacrificial butter—the two basic ritual offerings—with the myth of the churning rooted in the *havis* poured into the ritual fire. He thinks the ability of clarified butter to divide into parts as poured into fire (*amṛtam vipṛkvat*) is analogous to the stratification of the primal Ocean as it was churned, citing the mention of the sacred horse appearing "from the ocean, this primal source" in Hymn 163 of the first *maṇḍala* as auxiliary proof (*ṚV*.I.163.1). The scholar also singles out another stanza of this hymn, which points out that the steed was not merely born in the primal ocean but was "half divided from *soma*" (*asi somena samayā vipṛktaḥ*) (*ṚV*.I.163.3). Thus, the hymn includes the motif of oceanic birth, salient in the epic myth, and specifies its way, "division" designated by the verb describing the stratification of *Havis*.

As we see it, Geldner proposes the correct approach—Ṛgveda really offers the archaic precedent to the *Amṛtamanthana*. However, we discern an even closer Rgvedic parallel to this monument. By *amṛta*, the Veda means specially made *soma* juice, also granting immortality, no rarer than *Havis*. We think it was this circle of *amṛta* ideas that the myth of "The Churning of the Ocean" actualized. The epic myth closely follows the

Vedic idea of *amṛta* as *soma* juice. As the Ṛgveda specifies, the potion of immortality is to be found in water, and combines with medicines:

> "There is *amṛta* in the waters,
> There is a remedy in the waters,
> Be valiant, ye gods, for their glory."
> (*Ṛ*V.I.23.19)

There is a direct indication of the water provenance of *Amṛta*:

> "From the ocean rose the honeyed wave,
> Together with the Soma, it acquired the properties of *amṛta*."
> (*Ṛ*V.IV.58.1)

The epic myth also mentions *amṛta* concealed in water, to be separated by churning or powerful mixing. When the great Ocean was churned, "the gums of various trees and herbs mixed with the waters of the Ocean. And the celestials attained immortality by drinking the waters mixed with these gums vested with the properties of *amṛta*".[64] Thus, the myth also presupposes the idea of herbal juices diluted with water—the heart of the Vedic rite of *amṛta* making. The third component of *amṛta*—milk—is also present as part of the Ocean water turned into it when churned. Only *soma*, the principal ingredient of the elixir, is absent from the description, but the logic of the myth allows clear allusions to it with oblique characteristics instead of naming it. Among these oblique indications is the semantic renaming of *soma* into *amṛta*, and the untrivial device by which actual *Soma*-squeezing rites are presented at the mythological level.

Many Ṛgvedic hymns mention the *realia* of the ceremonial *soma*-making ritual, performed solely by priests. Only once does the Veda come across the rite of simple or urgent *soma* juice squeezing (*añjaḥsava*) to be performed by any householder with his wife (*ṚVI*.28). As we see it, the practical details of this Vedic rite, re-appraised as mythic events, lie at the basis of the *Amṛtamanthana*. Here is the Ṛgvedic description of the añjaḥsava rite:

"There where the broad-based stone is raised on high
to press [the juices] out,
O Indra, swallow [the juices] squeezed by the mortar."

"There where the woman performs now the pulling,
now the pushing [of the churn-staff],
O Indra, swallow [the juices] squeezed by the mortar."

"There where they tie the churn-staff
as reins to drive [a horse],
O Indra, swallow [the juices] squeezed by the mortar."*

(*Ṛ*V.I.28.1-4)

Coded in metaphors, this hymn, however, clearly points at devices and utensils which allow us to re-create the *soma*-squeezing process. A stone press was put to the bottom of a wooden mortar, with *soma* containing herbs on it. The churn-staff was tied with a rope, the head of the household and his wife gripping each end to pull at it in turn, thus making the staff rotate and mash the herbs, whose juice trickled into the mortar.

Notably, scholarly literature has ever yet described this rite, and translators of the hymn mostly interpret the word *manthā* as pestle[65] meaning that the herbs are not mashed but crushed—seemingly, a minor difference. In fact, it gives a different reconstruction of the quick *soma*-squeezing rite, based not on staff rotation but the up-and-down movements of the pestle as it is lifted and pushed down with an effort.

Be this as it may, the precise meaning of *manthā* is churn-staff, not pestle, as specially indicated by Sāyaṇa, author of the most authoritative Ṛgveda comments. As he stresses, *Pada* 4a of this hymn means the staff usually "used to mix milk [with *soma*]." The Vedic rite very rarely used pure *soma* juice. More often, it was diluted with water or cow milk by pouring

* *yatra grāva pṛthubudhna urdhvo bhavati sotave/*
ulūkhalasutānām aved indra jalgulaḥ//

yatra nāry apacyavam upacyavaṁ ca śikṣate/
ulūkhalasutānām aved indra jalgulaḥ//

yatra manthāṁ vibadhnate raśmīn yamitavā iva/
ulūkhalasutānām aved indra jalgulaḥ//

the juice, water and milk into a wooden vat and violently mixed with a churn-staff for the ritual potion. According to Sāyaṇa, the quick squeezing rite used the same utensils—evidently, with one difference—a pressing slab in the bottom. The rope fixing the *manthā* serves as another proof. This fixation is necessary for a staff; more than that, it is the basis of its work—while there is no point in tying a rope to a pestle. Symptomatically, the verb *"vibandh"*, used in this hymn, implies not mere tying but fixing on both ends[66]. In other words, the rope was to have both ends loose, with a special knot in the middle which tightly embraced the staff. The Ṛgveda compares this rope with reins tied to steer a horse—meaning that the staff was brought into motion with a rope. The wife of the master who performed the rite took one end, and he the other. Thus the utensil demanded not one person, as a pestle, but two.

Though there's a wealth of difference between *soma* squeezing in a little home mortar, and the cosmic scope of *amṛta* churning in the huge Ocean, it isn't hard to see that the resulting potion was practically the same. The myth we regard has the Ocean for the ritual vessel; associates the King Tortoise, who lies at the sea bottom giving his shelled back for the job, with the slab on the broad mortar bottom; and replaces the small churn-staff with the giant Mount Mandara, and the rope with Vāsuki. Like in the Vedic *añjaḥsava* rite, the grandiose Ocean contraption is set in motion by a rope pulled on both ends in turn.

The word *manthā,* used in the Ṛgvedic hymn we use for comparison, comes up here as a generic notion bringing together all actions involved in churning. Thus, *Mahābhārata* repeatedly refers to Mandara as *mantha-giri,* Mount Churn-staff, to Vāsuki as *manthaṇī-kṛta,* the Churner, and to water, as churned into milk by gods and demons, as *manthodaka* (i.e., *mantha-udaka*). The act of Ocean churning comes up as *manthana*—the word form used in the *Amṛtamanthana,* the name of the *Samavakāra*.

The imagery of the epic myth is also close enough to the Ṛgvedic. As the Veda has it, *soma* squeezing in a mortar is a very noisy process:

"If, O mortar, thou art set in every home,
There sound the loudest,
Like the drum of conquerors!"*

(*Ṛ*V.I.28.5)

Another sound effect accompanies the procuring of *amṛta* from the Ocean. When the gods and *Asura*s were churning the Ocean with Mandara, a great noise rose like thunder coming out of monstrous clouds.

In *Mahābhārata*, gods and demons turned Mandara at an amazing speed as they pulled now at Vāsuki's head, now tail. Similar movements made a churn-staff rotate on the bottom slab:

"These [both] who acquire by means of a sacrifice,
and obtain the best reward,
Rush loudly about, like two bay horses,
Devouring the herbs [of *soma*]."**

(*Ṛ*V.I.28.7)

The aerial turbulence produced by the rapid staff rotation is likened unto the wind. Likewise, the staff itself is addressed as a mighty tree:

"O Lord of the Forest,
The wind bloweth round thy top.
For Indra, press out, O mortar,
The *soma* to drink."***

(*Ṛ*V.I.28.6)

With flames and smoke, the winds accompanied Ocean churning to gather clouds round Mandara and pour rain on the heads of the tired celestial denizens.

The Ṛgvedic hymn shows how widespread the quick *soma* squeezing rite was, performed "in every home" (ṚV.I.28.5). We can thus assume that it was well known to all Indian

---

* *yac cid dhi tvaṁ gṛhegṛhe ulūkhalaka yujyase/*
iha dyumattamaṁ vada jayatām iva dundubhiḥ//

** *āyajī vājasātamā tā hy uccā vijarbhṛtaḥ/*
havī ivāndhāṁsi bapsatā//

*** *uta smate vanaspate vātaī vi vāti agram it/*
atho indrāya pātave sunu somaṁ ulūkhala//

social strata in the Vedic time—and the early epic period, judging by the persistence of Indian traditions. In other words, the mortar with a slab at the bottom, the churn-staff and the rope clearly indicated a particular *soma* rite. The mythic allegory was also meant to discern household utensils in the fantastic attributes of the cosmic churning, identical to them in function—the Tortoise with its rounded back corresponding closely enough to a slab; Mount Mandara, broad at the foot and peaking toward the top like a churn-staff; and Serpent Vāsuki, strong and elastic like a rope.

So, as we see it, the *Amṛtamanthana* reinterpreted the *soma* related Vedic cult ideas. Vedas practically omitted mythological treatment of the *soma* cult, giving pride of place to its ritual aspect. The *Amṛtamanthana* gave a new mythological interpretation, based on the initial Vedic symbolism actualized, to practical parts of the Vedic rites—*soma* squeezing and mixing the juice with water. *Soma* entered the epic tradition as *amṛta*, on the one hand, bringing out its unity with the Vedic symbol and, on the other, emphasizing its properties as immortality elixir.

In Hindu period *soma* and *amṛta* figured as partly interchangeable concepts, interconnected through the moon—the vessel preserving the immortality potion, and at the same time, identified with *Soma*, the moon god. This form of the *Soma* cult was not characteristic of the Vedic era. Thus, Vedic texts most often name the moon, *Candra*, not Soma. On the other hand, already the later Vedic time knew a widespread moon-*soma* connection. Thus, the rather late Ṛgvedic nuptial hymn, *of maṇḍala* X (*ṚV*.X.85), associated *Soma* with the moon; the Atharvaveda says that "the moon feeds on this [*soma*] potion, which consists of *amṛta*" (*Ath*.3.31.6); the *Śatapatha-Brāhmaṇa* steadily names the moon god, King *Soma*, the celestial food granting immortality, and the moon "the highest celestial glory of *Soma*" (*ŚBr*.VII.3.1.46). The *Śatapatha-Brāhmaṇa* directly indicates that "the moon is none other than King *Soma*, the food of gods" (*ŚBr*.XI.1.4.4). The *Aitareya-Brāhmaṇa* (*AitBr*.7.11.5) and many other Brāhmaṇas and Purāṇas offer a similar concept of the *Soma*-moon.

We see this concept of the *Soma*-moon-*amṛta* in the myth of

"The churning of the Ocean". According to tradition, *Soma*-moon, the firstborn of the cosmogonic creation, came out of the milk Ocean and rose to heaven. At the end of the myth, after they win the battle for *amṛta*, the gods put it in a formidable vessel and give it to Kṛtin-Nara to keep. *Mahābhārata* does not directly allude to the moon as this vessel, which it became as it emerged out of the churned Ocean. The later tradition, however, specified it as the vessel for the precious elixir. According to *Purāṇas*, the nighttime luminary was regularly filled with *amṛta* to be drunk by gods in the light half-month and *Pitṛs* in the dark. The interpretation of the *Soma* god as moon god and keeper of the *amṛta* was widespread in Hindu period, whereas the ritual hypostasis of *soma* as sacrificial juice lost all topicality. This change of symbolism was objectively due to the gradual obliteration of the *soma* cult in the later Vedic era. The epic time gave up rites of the *Somayajña* type, and even forgot the plant with its hallucinogenous juice. The sacral ideas of *soma*—the oldest kernel of the Indo-Aryan ritualism—were, nevertheless, holy enough in themselves to be fully forgotten. Probably, this was why the rites of *soma* squashing and mixing with milk and water, though leaving the everyday ritual system, received a mythological interpretation as the events that gave rise to the *Amṛtamanthana*.

Thus, the epic myth succeeded to many essential aspects of the Vedic *soma* concept, though its Vedic reminiscences are not limited to it. There is the motif of the god-demon battle—the central in the Vedic mythology. As *soma* embodied the principal Vedic rite, so the theme of gods-*Asura*s opposing was the principal Vedic myth. The Ṛgveda saw Indra as warrior god, and presented his duel with *Asura* in many versions of one and the same pattern. Essentially, *soma* was its indispensable attribute. *Soma* or *amṛta* is often presented as temporal possession of Indra's enemy, whom the god challenges to take over the precious elixir. Even more often, Soma is treated as Indra's ally promoting his victory (*ṚV*.IV.1-5). More than that, Indra always drinks *soma* before the battle and so comes out on top (*ṚV*.I.32.3). We can easily notice all these motives actualized in the *Amṛtamanthana*, where the fight starts for the wondrous potion, of which the gods partake before it, unlike the demons, to become deathless and the strongest, and thus rout their enemies.

As experts on Vedic mythology conclude, the Ṛgveda treated Indra's heroic fight with the *Asuras* as a creative act in which a harmonious Universe emerged out of the primogenital stagnant chaos[67]. The Vedic time also gave rise to the idea of a world born out of primal waters—the beginning of all things that exist (*ŚBr.*IV.7.4.3-5; IV.8.2.3-5). An analogous cosmogonic interpretation is met in the epic myth. Here, only the creative method is unique. The earlier tradition never mentioned a cosmos set in order by churning, which first coagulates the waters, then lending fabulous treasures and setting a new world order. The cosmogonic aspect of the *Amṛtamanthana* determined its outstanding impact on post-Vedic culture, which promoted it to the status of the pivotal Genesis tradition.

As we trace the links of this myth with Vedic mythology, we can't omit the motif of a woman stealing the magic elixir. The epic legend attaches pivotal significance to this act on the borderline between the two major events regarded above—the preparation of, and the battle for the *amṛta*. Curiously, this central episode is also borrowed from the Vedic mythic circle. The *Brāhmaṇas* include a legend of *soma* guarded by *Gandharvas*, and the gods gathering in conference to discuss how to get the potion. They adopted to many means, but to no result. At last, they said: "The *Gandharvas* are fond of women. Let us send *Vāc* (Speech) to them, and she returns to us together with *Soma*." This scheme proved a success as *Vāc* stole the elixir for the gods (*ŚBr.*III.2.4.1-4)[68]. This plot turn almost fully coincides with the *Amṛtamanthana*, where gods want to obtain *soma* from their rival friends and finally get it, using the mighty power of feminine charm. The epic legend makes this plot more complicated. It is not a goddess but Viṣṇu Nārāyaṇa figuring as a female who steals the immortality potion from the *Asuras*. The protagonist of the myth, he is addressed by gods for assistance at the critical instances of the churning. Notably, the female hypostasis is unique among the many *avatāras* of Viṣṇu, and connected with this myth alone. Possibly, his transformation into a beautiful woman was necessitated by a particular Vedic mythologeme according to which *soma* was stolen by a goddess.

As we see it, the epic *Amṛtamanthana* is a synthetic, artificially modelled myth which brought together the key ritual and mythological ideas of Vedism. The time of its origination remains a topical issue. As pointed out above, it was never registered in manuscripts of the Vedic era. Neither the Vedas nor the later *Brāhmaṇas* literature of the 8th and 7th centuries B.C. ever mentioned it. We first come across this legend in the opening book of *Mahābhārata*, whose mythology experts trace up to the oldest epic layer from about the mid-1st millennium B.C[69]. To all appearances, this date is a precise enough indication of the time when the myth emerged. Really, it appeared on the borderline of two eras—the later Vedic and the early epic. Notably, the type of mythological concepts and imagery are here closer to the old Veda texts than the *Brāhmaṇas* and *Upaniṣads*. The later Vedic writ preserves the theme of the god-*Asura* fight, but does not attach a cosmogonic content to it. The rivalry is treated with less solemnity, and the idea of struggle brought down. Thus, the *Upaniṣadic* prose, historically the closest to the earlier epic, tells of gods fighting demons with the help of *Udgītha*, peculiar ritual singing. The *Bṛhadāraṇyaka-Upaniṣad* has this to say: "Prajāpati gave birth to two kinds of beings—gods and *Asuras*. The gods were the younger, and *Asuras* the older. They grappled for these worlds. The gods said: 'Let us vanquish the *Asuras* by *Udgītha* during a sacrifice' " (*BṛUp*.1.3.1)[70]. The later Vedic era promoted this situation to an archetype. In fact, the gods' triumph now directly depended on their knowledge of *Brāhmaṇic* dogmatic norms and rites, in which they surpassed the *Asuras*. It is easy to see that the myth of *Amṛtamanthana* has nothing in common with this esoteric ritualized tradition. More than that, it negates this later, to an extent. The comparatively young *Mahābhārata* legend reflects another world view and contains an artificially revived archaic myth-making power.

We can thus state that a new myth arose in the Indian culture of the mid-1st millennium—a synthesis of the crucial ritual and mythological ideas of the Vedic time. *Mahābhārata* recorded its narrative variant, while the *Nāṭyaśāstra* prescribes its scenic practice, to which it traces the genesis of the performing tradition. The early drama immediately followed the *Pūrvaraṅga* on stage—a pivotal factor to bear in mind if we are to understand the goals of myth adaptation for the stage and to have a clearer idea of the status of this nascent drama. The legend of the first *Samavakāra* production directly specifies this order (*NŚ*.4.10). The drama could be performed only after the *Pūrvaraṅga* following all rules. Chapter I states this even more categorically: "Pitāmaha (Brahmā) said to all gods: 'Make a sacrifice in the playhouse in due order. Either the stage or the dramatic performance should not be held without the *pūjā*. And he who will hold the stage and the dramatic performance without the *pūjā* will find his knowledge useless and he will come to a bad rebirth. Whether it is the *Nartaka* (actor) or the *Arthapati* (his wealthy patron), if he does not perform the *pūjā* in accordance with conventions will attain auspicious wealth and [in the end] go to the celestial world" (*NŚ*.1.122-128).

So, according to the *Nāṭyaśāstra*, the rite and the drama are not merely closely interconnected: the mysterial action is practically pointless, even harmful, unless preceded by a particular sacrifice. The scenic myth not merely followed the *Pūrvaraṅga* but acquired a sacral status only as a complement to the strictly ordered rite. Possibly, the ritual tasks of the *pūjā* and the drama did not coincide. The esoteric message of the *pūjā* could be above the congregation's understanding, whereas the mythological content of the drama was clear to all. In other words, the *pūjā* was a liturgy addressed mainly to gods, while the scenic myth played the part of a visual sermon intended for an impact on the worshippers. Thus the drama played a major ritual and homiletic part as acquainting believers with the canonical tradition.

In fact, the *Pūrvaraṅga* and the *Nāṭya* together formed a unique liturgical sequence in which the former had the function of the liturgy, with its ordered ritual patterns, and framed the *pūjā*, sacrificial sacrament, while the *Nāṭya* that followed had the status of liturgical drama. Though appearing together in one sacred ceremony, the rite and the ritual drama were autonomous enough as related to each other. The *Pūrvaraṅga-pūjā* had a universal message, as shown in Chapter I of this study. A rite with a pre-set and unchanged theological basis, it could be performed even without its drama complement—as, for instance, in the medieval *pūjā*—whereas the early drama was, to all appearances, impossible outside the ceremonial worship, and was enacted only in the sacrificial process.

Close interaction of the *Pūrvaraṅga* and the *Nāṭya* resulted in a number of ritual and mythological ideas which the rite and the ritual drama shared. Thus, as we analysed the epic tradition, we pointed out the unique transformation of Viṣṇu into a beautiful woman, which stands out in the mythology of this god and is connected with the *Amṛtamanthana*. We can't but notice in this connection that the *Pūrvaraṅga* also worshipped Viṣṇu in his female hypostasis. The three steps of the *Sūtradhāra* were addressed in adoration to Viṣṇu as carrying the female element, Brahmā in the impersonal neuter hypostasis, and Śiva the male (*NŚ*.5.98-101). Considering the non standard femininity of Viṣṇu, we can explain the coded symbolism of the priest's performance only by the particular episode in the *Amṛtamanthana* which gave substantiation to the unique *avatāra* of the multifaced god.

This similarity of the *Pūrvaraṅga* and the *Amṛtamanthana* is not the only one. There are other ample coincidences, among them the semantics of the white colour. White flowers were scattered on the stage during the *Pūrvaraṅga*, with its white-clad priests. Notably, the fabulous wealth acquired during Ocean churning is also white, as are the *Soma*, moon, the raiment of goddess Śrī, the steed *Uccaiḥśravas* and, last but not least, the radiant vessel in which *amṛta* appeared from the Ocean. Evidently, white outwardly symbolized godhead and the immaculate purity of the celestial world, and so prevailed in the colour scheme of the rite and the stage myth.

Probably, the content of the earliest *Samavakāra* not merely had an impact on the *Pūrvaraṅga* symbolism but largely influenced the evolution of the narrative variant of the *Amṛtamanthana*, as gone down to us in *Mahābhārata*. In this sense, not the drama used the epic legend but the scenic myth determined the emergence of the legend in *Mahābhārata*, which preserved some of its genre traits even in the epic form.

* * *

There is another important question—of the performers of the scenic myth. As we see it, at first these were the four priests who performed the *Pūrvaraṅga*. This is not a vain supposition, as borne out by the testimony of medieval theoreticians, above all, Abhinavagupta. His comments on the *Nāṭyaśāstra* contain a direct indication that four personages were to appear in each act of the *Samavakāra*—the protagonist, his opponent and two assistants (*AbhBh*, vol.II, p.437). This opinion has support from other drama experts. We meet a similar statement in the *Nāṭyadarpaṇa*, among others (*ND*, p.109).

At first sight, this testimony made by medieval theoreticians contradicts the *Nāṭyaśāstra*, which indicates the number of *Samavakāra* characters as twelve. However, the text does not specify whether they appeared all together in every act or were distributed among the acts on one condition, that their total number remain unchanged. If we suppose that there was an equal number of characters in all three *Samavakāra* parts—four—and multiply this number by three, the number of parts, we get the figure mentioned by the *Nāṭyaśāstra*.

If this assumption is correct, the priests were to leave the stage for a short while after the *Pūrvaraṅga* to make themselves up and put on the appropriate costumes to appear as celestial beings not in the mediated form of the *Pūrvaraṅga* but openly—two as gods and the other two as *Asuras*, their rivals.

The early drama had a sacral, rather than spectacular message. So, evidently, its performers not so much imitated their divine prototypes as were temporarily reincarnated as these. We can easily imagine an audience perceiving the persons on stage not as humans dressed and made up as gods but the deities themselves, who appeared before the worshippers in visual form. The congregation must have been deeply moved to see Brahmā, Viṣṇu Nārāyaṇa and other gods in the flesh as they performed the *Amṛtamanthana*. The idiom of imagery, understood by all, promoted the popularity of the pious ideas underlying the myth. Based on a combination of strongly transformed Vedic archetypes, this myth was at once new and recognisable as it revealed to the congregation the mysteries of the Genesis and the creation of the cosmic order as seen by the priests who performed the scenic *pūjā*.

Possibly, the oldest forms of this religious ceremony, which consisted of a *pūjā* and a *Nāṭya*, were simple enough. Much time was to pass before it acquired the subtle and precise form we know from the *Nāṭyaśāstra*. We can now reconstrue with any degree of probability only this developed stage of the evolving tradition, with the ten-part scenic *Pūrvaraṅga*, whose final part hinted at the topic of the play, to be followed by the three acts of the *Samavakāra*. As we see it, in this case the author of the treatise made precise characteristics of the archaic scenic performance, with its pre-set length and strictly ordered themes, instead of formulating general characteristics of the genre which had a certain variability. This reglamentation hardly had an artistic goal, but it excellently corresponded to the temporal and contextual norm of the rite.

As we see it, the *Samavakāra* was the basic and oldest type of mystery drama—a stage version of a cosmogonic myth which appeared in the middle of the 1st millennium B.C. As visual sermon, it was part and parcel of a divine service in the *pūjā* form, and was performed by the priests involved in the sacrifice. As the *Pūrvaraṅga*, which brought *dharma*, fame and longevity (*NŚ*.5.57), the *Samavakāra* was a unique rite which, as the *Nāṭyaśāstra* pointed out, helped to achieve three basic goals in life—*dharma*, *kāma* and *artha* (*NŚ*.4.3).

ḌIMA. THE MYTH OF THE BURNING OF TRIPURA

Ḍima, the mysterial drama closest to the *Samavakāra*, comes up in Chapter IV of the *Nāṭyaśāstra* as the world's second drama, composed by Brahmā right after the *Amṛtamanthana*. According to its title, the *Tripuradāha*, it presented "The Burning of Tripura". Most probably, it really appeared somewhat later than *Samavakāra* to reflect the next and close stage of tradition evolution. As the type of ritual drama we have regarded, the *Ḍima* was part of a religious ceremony with a permanent obligatory part, the *Pūrvaraṅga*, and a changeable *Nāṭya* (*NŚ*.4.9). Evidently, the scenic sermons could be varied, unlike the liturgy, with various myths enacted after one and the same rite. As we see it, *Ḍima* can hardly be classified as drama proper—just as *Samavakāra*. They both rather represented theatrical forms immobile and stringent enough, with all characteristics determined by the plot of the basic myth. The content and structure of these protodramatic forms were closely interlinked. As a result, the events in the legend of "The burning of Tripura" did not fit into the three-part *Samavakāra*. To all appearances, a particular kind of drama was specially made for it to fix the distinctive features of the scenic representation of this myth.

Chapter XX gives *Ḍima* far more concise and general characteristics than *Samavakāra*: "*Ḍima* is a play that consists of four parts and contains six *Rasas*. The plot is well known and the hero is a renowned personality of an exalted (*Udātta*) type. Excluding the *Hāsya* (comic) and *Śṛṅgāra* (erotic), the other *Rasas* are represented. The plot has the exciting *Rasas* and various *Bhāvas* brightly displayed. Incidents like thunderstorm, earthquake (*Nirghāta)*, fall of meteors, eclipses of the sun or the moon, fights, wrestling, challenging and mutual conflicts should be included. Acts of deceit, jugglery, etc. are brought in profusely. There are energetic activities of many persons and dissention (*Bheda*) among themselves. Gods, *Asuras*, *Rākṣasas*, *Bhūtas*, *Yakṣas* and *Nāgas* predominate; as many as sixteen heroes should be carefully made in the *Sāttvatī* and *Ārabhaṭī Vṛttis*, and different *Bhāvas* are to be resorted to supplement these" (*NŚ*.20.84-89). As the treatise has it, this drama had four acts. The *Nāṭyaśāstra* says nothing about their plots and length, though specifying the number of characters—perhaps, of major significance. Thus, *Ḍima* was an act longer than *Samavakāra*, with four characters more. This was hardly a chance numerical coincidence. Most probably, it was acted out by the four priests who performed the *pūjā* and appeared in the *Samavakāra*. They all appeared on stage in every *Ḍima* act—hence the greater overall number of characters.

The other definitions of the treatise describe not the structure but the content of *Ḍima*. Gods, *Asuras*, *Rākṣasas*, *Bhūtas*, *Yakṣas* and *Nāgas* were its heroes, all of divine or demonic nature. The protagonist, who stood out among them, belonged to the *Udātta*, sublime type. There were no females either among the characters or the performers. The plot was to be derived from mythology and be of common knowledge, always based on a conflict, *Bheda*, which led to clashes, duels, mutual deceptions and intrigues among the parties at odds. Played both in the *Sāttvatī* and *Ārabhaṭī Vṛttis*, *Ḍima* was closer oriented on battle scenes than *Samavakāra*. Expressive and full of suspense, this dark drama had no erotic and comic elements, as the *Nāṭyaśāstra* pointed out, with an emotional scheme based on the six other *Rasas*. The action led the heroes and the audience through sadness, wrath, courage, fear, revulsion and astonishment—in this or any other succession. The treatise prescribed to *Ḍima* not only battle but storms, earthquakes, falling meteorites, lunar and solar eclipses and other calamities, which, no doubt, demanded movable props and sophisticated dummies. Its scenery was surely not only sumptuous and colourful but technically subtle.

However schematic and conventionalized this description may be, it gives an idea of the *Ḍima* structure and content clear enough to compare it with the myth of "The burning of Tripura". The *Nāṭyaśāstra* does not retell it, but we can find it in *Mahābhārata* alongside with the *Amṛtamanthana*. The *Karṇaparva*, Book VIII of the epic, tells of this demonic fortress which Śiva reduced to ashes with an arrow[71]. Here is its gist.

In times immemorial, after the gods vanquished the *Asuras* and threw them into the ocean, three sons of Taraka, the demon chose the way of ascesis. Many years of piety earned them Brahmā's favour, and they asked the Lord to allow them to build a fortress which nothing and no one could destroy. Brahmā said that everything in the world was fated to death and destruction, but they could build three cities which would never fall unless they merged into one. Guided by Maya, the *Asura* architect, the demons built these three cities—the first, of gold, in heaven, another, silver, hovering in the air, and the third, iron, standing firm on earth. After this, they became the scourge of all denizens of the three worlds.

Led by Indra, the gods came to Brahmā for advice. To protect them and punish the iniquitous demons, Brahmā told them to turn to mighty Śiva, to whom the gods addressed praises and the request to destroy Tripura. Śiva lent them a benevolent ear and agreed to this feat of might and glory, if every god gave him half of his magic power. They agreed and made him the strongest of all, with the name of Mahādeva, Great God.

A wondrous chariot was made for the battle. The Earth

goddess with her large cities, her mountains and forests and islands that house diverse creatures was made the car, Mount Mandara and the great Ocean the axles, Vāsuki the reins, Sun and Moon wheels, and the firmament, with all its stars and planets, tent. Mount Meru became the flagstaff, and clouds, multi-coloured banners. The year, with its six seasons, served as a bow, and three great gods took positions in an all-destructive arrow—*Agni* became its staff, *Soma* head, and Viṣṇu point.

The chariot made, *Apsara*s danced in Śiva's honour to the accompaniment of *Gandharvas'* music. Everything was ready for the battle but for the driver. Brahmā took this place on all celestial beings' request. Calamities shook the three worlds as soon as the cosmic chariot moved. The demonic cities came a tremble as it approached, and as soon as they came together, Śiva's arrow set them aflame.

It is easy to see the parts into which this myth falls, like the *Amṛtamanthana*—each resembling an act in a play. The first tells of the demons' ascesis and the building of Tripura. Next goes the episode when the gods ask Brahmā and then Śiva to destroy Tripura. The next is wholly devoted to the making of Śiva's cosmic chariot. The great battle ending with the *Asura* fortress burned crowns the action.

On the whole, the myth follows the *Ḍima* criteria closely enough. It retells a well-known story borrowed from epic mythology and based on a god-demon conflict leading to clashes and life-and-death battles. All characters were either deities or demons. One stood out among them—a sublime protagonist—as the *Nāṭyaśāstra* prescribed. Śiva Mahādeva alone could aspire to this part after the others made him Great God.

The plot of the Tripura myth followed the *Ḍima* characteristics in another aspect, too: it did not involve female characters and comic or love scenes. A serious epic legend, dramatic and elevated, it was centered round the culminating moment, when Tripura was given to fire. The events fell in two parts. Whatever preceded the battle must have been enacted in the *Sāttvatī Vṛtti,* with battle preparations, especially the chariot making, meant to raise the martial spirit of Śiva and intimidate his *Asura* opponents. *Ārabhaṭī Vṛtti,* the other style prescribed by the *Nāṭyaśāstra* for *Ḍima*, must have been employed in the battle scene. As the treatise points out, the stage version of the *Tripuradāha* required a wealth of props and dummies. Possibly, the three cities symbolizing the earthly, airy and celestial worlds were present on stage at different levels. There must have been a likeness of Śiva's chariot, which received its cosmic attributes and decorations—tents and banners—before the audience's eyes. Possibly, when the action climaxed, the vehicle was set in motion to start a series of stage effects imitating lunar and solar eclipses, a shower of meteors, earthquakes and other dreadful calamities which *Ḍima* demanded. The culmination could also spectacularly represent the three cities brought to the same level to merge into one and meet its fate with Śiva's fiery arrow.

We can, probably, fully rely on the *Nāṭyaśāstra* in its legendary testimony to assume that the protodramatic genre of *Ḍima* was related to this epic myth, mentioned in the treatise. In other words, the *Ḍima Tripuradāha* really existed and was enacted during solemn worship, like the *Amṛtamanthana*. The mutual closeness of the corresponding epic myths in imagery and narration structure is characteristic in this sense. Both use the same symbolic images—Mounts Mandara and Meru, serpent Vāsuki and others. The action of the *Tripuradāha* unfolds in the mythological Universe where the *Amṛtamanthana* events took place. Each myth gives a different interpretation to the one battle mythologem, with concrete events serving to glorify the two supreme Hindu deities—Viṣṇu in the *Amṛtamanthana*, and Śiva in the *Tripuradāha*. Even more important is the echo of these epic myths, mentioned as the oldest dramas, in the ritualistic and mythological information of the *Nāṭyaśāstra*. We have pointed out the link between the *Samavakāra Amṛtamanthana* and the *Pūrvaraṅga*. The *Ḍima Tripuradāha* offers analogous parallels to *Nāṭyaśāstra* rites. Thus, when the *Ācārya* worshipped the many gods in the theatre consecration, he adored Siva in the hypostasis of the destroyer of Tripura, addressing him with the following mantra: "O God of Gods, great god Gaṇeśa, thou who ended the Tripura, accept this oblation purified by the mantra, O God prosperous in *māyā*" (*NŚ*.3.47). Significantly, as he glorified the gods, the priest usually named the most salient feature or most glorious deed of each, and the *Nāṭyaśāstra* singled out one—connected with "The Burning of Tripura"—of Śiva's many feats in its ritual-mythological system.

Perfectly suited for Śiva worship, the myth was narrated in this form in the *Śaiva Purāṇas*, younger than *Mahābhārata*—a fact which allowed experts to assume that the adoration of Śiva as God of gods, with even Brahmā ousted into the background, was due to confessional orientations of the *Purāṇa* authors[72]. However, the epic myth has about the same spirit, with Śiva as supreme god and pillar of other gods' well-being. He rivals Brahmā in might, and is superior to him in some aspects. Most probably, the Tripura myth had this Śaivite slant from the start, rather than came with a later reinterpretation.

The unique status of Śiva in the epic myth is similar to his elevated position in the *Nāṭyaśāstra* legend on the origin of *Ḍima* — a very characteristic factor. According to this tradition, *Śiva* did not appear at the *Amṛtamanthana* premiere, which gathered all gods and demons. To make him see it, Brahmā and the other gods went to his Himalayan abode to repeat the performance for him. They greeted Śiva, and Brahmā addressed him with the following speech: "O best and most excellent one among the *Suras*, it behoves you to grant me the favour [of] seeing and hearing the *Samavakāra* composed by me" (*NŚ*.4.7). Śiva agreed to attend the performance, and also saw the *Pūrvaraṅga* preceding it. As the legend has it, the *Nāṭya* was immediately followed by another, written by Brahmā specially for Śiva and his retinue of *Bhūta*s and *Gaṇas*—a *Ḍima* named *Tripuradāha*, which Śiva and his companions liked immensely (*NŚ*.4.5-10).

As we easily notice, the circumstances of this performance repeat, in a sense, the plot of the Tripura myth. Like the epic tradition, the *Nāṭyaśāstra* legend presents Śiva as standing above the other gods, and Brahmā emphasizes his dependence on him, not so much inviting Śiva to see the play as asking him to condescend to see and hear it. To mollify the awesome god, Brahmā and other celestial beings worship him, as did the gods who asked him to protect them from *Asura*s in the epic myth.

Brahmā addresses Śiva as the greatest drama expert, who

can pronounce the right judgement on the art of *Nāṭya*, which Brahmā invented. As is generally accepted, Śiva saw only one drawback in it, which he corrected by adding dance to the spectacle. This universally acknowledged assumption is met both in reviews of the Oriental theatre and special studies of the Sanskrit drama. In reality, however, this interpretation of the *Nāṭyaśāstra* legend is not wholly correct. The treatise really says that upon seeing the *Nāṭya*, Śiva recalled the dancing movements and poses he had invented in times immemorial—"during the time of duck" (*NŚ*.4.13)—perhaps, meaning *Pralaya*, whose advent was directly connected with his orgiastic *Tāṇḍava* dance, the end of the Universe. Eager to share his dancing expertise, Śiva, however, thought that it ought to enrich not the *Nāṭya* but the preceding *Pūrvaraṅga* rite. "Let this [dance] be used by thou, [O Brahmā,] in the *Pūrvaraṅga*, in the application of the *Vardhamānaka* in regard to the *Gītas*, *Āsāritas* and *Mahāgītas* to duly portray the content [of the songs with the help of dance movements]. The *Pūrvaraṅga* that has [just] been performed by you is *Śuddha* (pure), but on being combined with this [dance] they (*Pūrvaraṅgas*) will become *Citra* (ornate) by name" (*NŚ*.4.14-16). As we thus see from the context, the religious ceremony performed before the *Amṛtamanthana* and *Tripuradāha*, and shown to Śiva with the dramas, did not include dancing, and so was classified as *Śuddha*, pure. It was precisely the one that Śiva decided to embellish with an interlude dance, which ought to repeat the content of the songs which sounded at the very start of the scenic part of the *Pūrvaraṅga*, even before the *Sūtradhāra* and his two assistants appeared on the stage (*NŚ*.4.14-15). To tell this *Pūrvaraṅga* from the earlier, it received a new name—*Citra*. This legendary testimony must be correct to describe the *Śuddha Pūrvaraṅga* as older than the *Citra*. Notably, the instance which Śiva points out for dancing exactly corresponds to the priestesses' interlude. Most probably, the female dance worship was added to the *Pūrvaraṅga* rather late—at any rate, when the rite had its basic structure fully shaped and established. It was glued on to the start of the scenic part of the *Pūrvaraṅga* without any influence on the further development of the ritual events. In fact, this legend of the *Nāṭyaśāstra* not merely retells the origin of a more spectacular *Pūrvaraṅga* but substantiates female participation, as the *Śuddha Pūrvaraṅga* required only the male priests. This was how the rite plus dance became *Citra* not only in terms of expressive means but of performers. In other words, Śiva, who taught the actors dancing, can be called the author of a special kind of *Pūrvaraṅga*—not a new type of drama including dances among its many components.

Thus, the mythological content of the epic contains a legend which elevates Śiva as God of gods at the top of the celestial hierarchy. At the same time, *Nāṭyaśāstra* rites worship him in the hypostasis of the destroyer of Tripura. Doubtless, the *Tripuradāha*—the plot of the ancient *Ḍima*—and the ritual-mythological spectacles presented by the treatise did not take shape irrespective of each other, but rather came out of one and the same source within one religious system.

In this connection, we need at least a concise analysis of the origin of the *Tripuradāha*. Like the *Amṛtamanthana*, it has pronounced Vedic reminiscences. Even the Vedas include fragmented legends of *Asuras*' fortified cities in the three worlds. Judging by its numerous mentions, this myth was also rather popular in the later Vedic era (*TaitSam*.6.2.3; *MaitSam*.3.8.1; *AitBr*.4.6.8; *ŚBr*.III.4.4). The *Brāhmaṇas* retell it in a very concise form, saying only that once upon a time, the gods contended with the *Asuras* for lordship over the worlds. The demons built three strongholds—iron on earth, silver in the air and gold in heaven. Later, the gods came together and determined to vanquish the demons, for which they chose a telling way—to besiege the fortresses with a special sacrifice (*ŚBr*.III.4.3.4). A description of the rite follows as performed by gods and known as the *Upāsad*, lit., Siege.

The *Upāsad* was part of the *Pravargya* rite, with special stress on the worship of three gods—*Agni*, *Soma* and Viṣṇu, in whose honour Ṛgvedic hymns were recited and the *Upāsad Homa*, oblations and clarified butter, were sacrificed to the three. The rite repeated twice a day—in the morning and afternoon—for three days running. The priests' oblation offerings and praises of *Agni*, *Soma* and Viṣṇu were interpreted as symbolizing the siege of cities. These *Brāhmaṇic* interpretations reveal the esoteric meaning of this rite, whose destructive power was likened unto the arrow in whose parts the three gods were embodied (*AitBr*.4.6.8)[73].

Thus, the later Vedic era interpreted the Tripura legend in the *Brāhmaṇic* spirit to explain a particular rite. Evidently, the *Mahābhārata* myth is far enough from its Vedic sources, to which it owes only the basic plot lines and the idea of three cities destroyed with an arrow in which *Agni*, *Soma* and Viṣṇu were embodied, the rest being wholly original. Śiva was promoted to protagonist. The god-*Asura* rivalry from ritualised became cosmic, and a colourful description of chariot-making and other martial preparations took up the bulk of the narration. As the *Amṛtamanthana*, the epic myth of *Tripuradāha* is synthetic, with diverse Vedic motifs merging—as, for instance, the features of Rudra, Śiva's Vedic prototype, who excelled in archery and never parted with bow-and-arrows. He owned the chariot used in many battles. The Vedic Tripura legend does not mention this vehicle, whereas the epic version presents it as analogous to the Universe, giving its cosmogonic description a value unto its own.

Importantly, the very title of the legendary *Ḍima* allows us to see which of the myth—the Vedic or the epic—received a scenic treatment in the *Tripuradāha* as it alludes not merely to the destruction but to the burning of Tripura. This motif of the triple city reduced to ashes was unknown in the Vedic versions, appearing only in *Mahābhārata*, where Śiva burned the *Asura* fortresses with an arrow of fire. Thus we can see that the *Ḍima Tripuradāha* proceeded from the epic version. Like the *Amṛtamanthana*, it could not appear earlier than the mid-1st millenium B.C., considered to be the time when the oldest layer of *Mahābhārata* took shape. We cannot rile out that here, too, the narrative version of the myth, as preserved in the epic, left a considerable influence of the ritual drama which re-interpreted the Vedic myth of the three fortified cities of the *Asuras*.

To sum up this issue, we ought to notice the vital observations following from our contextual analysis of the mystery drama in its oldest forms. In both cases, the plot of the myth adapted for the stage emerged out of reinterpreted Vedic cult ideas. Both myths were unknown as complete narrations in the Vedic era to appear as late as the epic time. The *Amṛtamanthana* and the *Tripuradāha* are close to each other as far as their imagery and manner of narration goes. At the same time, the ritual-mythological complex of the *Nāṭyaśāstra* offers direct parallels to religious ideas which make them unique. We see it as proof of both the ritual texts of the treatise and the two myths we have here regarded belonging to one ritual-mythological system with sacral dramatic performances as is crucial distinctive feature.

ĪHĀMṚGA AND *VYĀYOGA*

Two other *Āviddha* dramas, the *Īhāmṛga* and the *Vyāyoga*, are close to the basic types of the ritual drama, *Samavakāra* and *Ḍima*. Scanty extant information about their structure only mentions that the *Vyāyoga* had only one act and "like the *Samavakāra*, [involved] numerous male characters, but in a shorter action, for [the *Vyāyoga*] had only one part" (*NŚ*.20.92). The treatise does not specify the number of acts in the *Īhāmṛga* but points out that "all precepts concerning the *Vyāyoga* are as valid for the *Īhāmṛga*, [including characters] men, the styles and the *Rasas*" (*NŚ*.20.81). If we follow these *Nāṭyaśāstra* precepts, we can assume that the similarity of these two drama types also concerned the number of acts, i.e., the *Īhāmṛga* was a one-act play, too. Later, medieval treatises referred to an *Īhāmṛga* of four acts, but the *Nāṭyaśāstra* appears to mean a shorter play. Otherwise, it is hard to see why the authors of the *Nāṭyaśāstra* omitted the number of acts—a crucial characteristic—and failed to describe the inner structure in their canonical definition of the drama type.

Proceeding from all this, we can assume that the *Īhāmṛga* and the *Vyāyoga* had more in common than only dramatis personae, *Vṛttis* (representation style) and *Rasas*, emotions evoked in the audience—but they had the same number of acts. In the oldest dramas, trilogies and tetralogies, number and length of parts made up for the unsophisticated structure of each particular act. Unlike them, the one-act *Īhāmṛga* and *Vyāyoga* had an elaborate form. The *Nāṭyaśāstra* specially stresses the structural perfection of these genres. Thus, a well-made plot (*suvihitavastunibandha*) made the *Īhāmṛga* highly convincing (*NŚ*.20.78) as based on traditional history—a myth adapted for the stage. This drama needed unblemished composition (*susamāhitakāvyabandha*) (*NŚ*.20.80)—which, in a one-act play, mainly implied a well-arranged division into scenes and episodes which joined in an unbroken line of action. Unity of time is introduced into the definition of the *Vyāyoga*. According to the *Nāṭyaśāstra*, it was to represent events taking place within a day (*NŚ*.20.90).

Doubtless, the *Īhāmṛga* and the *Vyāyoga* emerged later than the *Samavakāra* and the *Ḍima* to represent the next developmental stage of the mysterial theatre. We can only guess which practical steps determined the progress of the drama. Most probably, this evolution gradually complicated the structure of every act within the oldest many-act dramas. With all canonical features preserved, the inner composition of an act was improved to receive a more harmonious structure and enrich itself with diverse novelties of a purely theatrical nature. We shall also bear in mind that the *Samavakāra* had only formal connections between its parts which, in fact, were three independent plays. Possibly, the form of one of them lent its pattern to a new kind of the one-act play at a definite stage of the theatrical evolution, with reglamentation not so strict than in the archaic mysterial genres.

Unlike the *Samavakāra* and the *Ḍima*, the *Nāṭyaśāstra* does not contain any direct indications of the myths on which the *Īhāmṛga* and the *Vyāyoga* were based, though providing detailed enough characteristics of their content. The *Īhāmṛga* described gods' feud for the love of a celestial maiden. The conflict brewed round her wrath, which sent the heroes into panic, *Saṃkṣobha*, excitement, *Vidrava*, and mutual strife, *Saṃpheṭa* (*NŚ*.20.70). The plot revolved round an amorous intrigue which resulted in struggle for the heroine, her abduction and a clash (*NŚ*.20.80).

The characters, of celestial origin, were all endowed with fiery (*Uddhata*) passions and unbridded temperament. As the action unfolded, they kindled the flame of mutual hatred which climaxed in a scenic battle (*NŚ*.20.82).

To all appearances, the *Īhāmṛga* enacted a particular myth or several myths connected with a chase after an antelope, as the name of the genre shows: *īha*, 'attempt', 'catch', and *mṛga*, 'antelope'. Among others, they could include the myth of *Dakṣa*'s sacrifice. According to the myth *Dakṣa* called all gods to take part in the first-ever ritual offering he was making. Śiva, the only exception, had no part in the sacrifice. Enraged, he came to the site with his bow, pierced the sacrificial being with an arrow, and it took the form of an antelope and soared to heaven to become the constellation *Mṛgaśīrṣa*, antelope's head.

This mythic version does not wholly coincide with formal criteria of the *Īhāmṛga* plot. In particular, it leaves no room for a love affair. Nevertheless, we should not discard it because it deals with an antelope chase and, more than that, comes up in the *Nāṭyaśāstra* to substantiate the appearance of the *Tāṇḍava*, which Śiva danced after he destroyed *Dakṣa*'s offering (*NŚ*.4.255).

Another version of this tradition is offered by the myth of *Prajāpati*, who assumed the disguise of an antelope buck to commit incest with his daughter. For this outrage, Śiva severed his head, which turned into the *Mṛgaśīrṣa* constellation for all times. Possibly, there were more variants of the myth, which followed this pattern: Śiva, the protagonist, flew into rage for some reason or other and came out for justice, performing a feat of glory which resulted in a new constellation, the *Mṛgaśīrṣa*, appearing in the sky. The *Īhāmṛga* might include one or several variants of this myth, whose generic name, the antelope chase, came to denote a dramatic genre.

The plot of the *Vyāyoga* has not come down to us. As in other *Āviddha* dramas, the action was set in motion by conflicts between the characters, which brewed bitter clashes, duels and, finally, a stage battle which involved all dramatis personae (*NŚ*.20.93). The treatise does not add anything on this account. A protagonist well known from legends stood out among the male heroes—notably, not a god but a sage of royal blood (*NŚ*.20.92). This preference of a mortal to a divine protagonist runs counter to the rule followed by all *Āviddha* dramas as centered only round gods and demons. This discrepancy can have many explanations. From these we single out one, which we see as the most probable. As all ritual dramas, the *Vyāyoga* initially revolved round a celestial being later substituted by a mortal. This assumption is borne out by a number of medieval treatises which, to all appearances, echoed an earlier tradition and prescribed a deity as *Vyāyoga* hero (*BhPr*, p.248.8; *SD*, p.233). Evidently, one particular stage in the drama evolution made heroes' godhead no longer obligatory. At any rate, they allowed a mortal protagonist in the *Īhāmṛga* (*SD*, p.246; *DR*.III.64-67). Most probably, this was a rather recent substitute. At any rate, it shows that the original message of the ritual drama was largely committed to oblivion. Whereas the ancient *Nāṭya* retold conflicts between gods and *Asuras*, and the suprapersonal nature of its heroes was a crucial matter, the classical period of dramatic evolution made it more natural to introduce this-worldly characters.

Unlike the *Samavakāra* and the *Dima*, the *Īhāmṛga* and the *Vyāyoga* included female characters—another indication of their comparatively recent appearance. The heroine of the *Īhāmṛga* played a pivotal part in the centre of a dramatic intrigue where she personified discord (*NŚ*.20.78). The *Vyāyoga* did not demand a woman protagonist, involving, nevertheless, several female characters (*NŚ*.20.90)—most probably, in background episodes. They hardly needed to be celestial creatures. Here, in particular, lay the vital difference between the *Vyāyoga* and the *Īhāmṛga*, necessarily centered round a goddess (*NŚ*.20.81).

The introduction of female characters did not seriously influence the imagery of the ritual drama, wholly subjected to the pathos of the mysterial battle. The martial plays gave a better part of the scenic time to clashes between gods and *Asuras*, and women made do with supporting parts. Even in its general definition of *Āviddha* dramas, the *Nāṭyaśāstra* points out women's stage presence as something non-intrinsic to these *Nāṭyas*. They were not numerous and did not take active participation in plot development.

In itself, the appearance of women in one-act *Nāṭyas* does not mean that they had a lesser sacral status than *Samavakāra* and *Ḍima*. In the *Nāṭyaśāstra* rites—mainly the *Pūrvaraṅga*—involved priestesses on a par with male priests. Possibly, the more archaic *Śuddha Pūrvaraṅga*, involving men alone, took shape in the oldest era of *Samavakāra* and *Ḍima* performances, while the *Citra* was directly linked to *Īhāmṛga* and *Vyāyoga* types. It is difficult to say in which female performers appeared the earliest, and whether the arrangement came to the rite from the ritual drama or, the other way round, came to the *Nāṭya* from the *Pūrvaraṅga*. Most probably, the process was reciprocal, and the innovations which conditioned the appearance of the *Citra Pūrvaraṅga*, at the same time, determined the appearance of one-act drama genres in which women could act side-by-side with men. No doubt, the introduction of female characters allowed to give a variety to the topics treated on stage, and add tension and suspense to the plays. The emergence of the new drama varieties hardly meant that the *Samavakāra* and the *Ḍima* disappeared altogether. More probably, shorter plays accompanied the many-act archaic dramas. In these concise dramas, the playwriting craft of the ritual theatre reached its climax. At the same time, they spelt its decline.

The ritual performance following the *Pūrvaraṅga* was meant for innumerable repetitions in one and the same form. Consequently, the mystery drama needed several centuries to form its pivotal scenic principles within the framework of a ritual canon, with its inner resistance to active innovation. Nevertheless, as far as we can judge by the *Nāṭyaśāstra*, the ancient Indian ritual theatre made tremendous progress, with a system of basic ritual genres, a sophisticated gesticular idiom, and symbolism of make-up and costumes. Cult theatricals employed props and variegated stage effects. There was musical accompaniment and dance based on a canonical set of movements and refined mimicry. In other words, the process of ritual acting brought a wealth of purely theatrical discoveries and unique performing techniques. These were inherited by the Sanskrit literary drama, whose earliest samples, from the first centuries A.D., owed their perfect structure to the centuries-old progress of the *Nāṭya* within the framework of ritual ceremonies. Whereas religious spectacles resulted from a collective effort of the priesthood, as it sought to preserve and pass on forms sanctified by tradition, the literary genres born outside the religious rite proved far freer and more mobile.

Classic Sanskrit dramas had one salient feature which brought them close together between themselves and walled them off from mystery plays. This was their self-sufficiency as spectacles which pursued no longer a sacral but a pure aesthetic result. They were meant not to preach but to entertain. This was the goal of all expressive means which the secular theatre inherited from the mysterial stage.

As the *Nāṭaka* and *Prakaraṇa* genres transformed the drama from religious performance into court or city entertainment, it lost many of its ritual functions but found a new life in the centuries of Sanskrit stage classics. However, the classical theatre is outside this study, aimed to demonstrate the ritual character of the early drama. Both its content (myths), characters (gods and demons) and function (visual sermon) made it a unique rite, part and parcel of ceremonial worship as started in the *pūjā* form.

CHAPTER III

THE RITUAL DRAMA IN EARLY HINDU CULTURE

After we have studied the ritual system accompanying the ancient mystery performances and demonstrated the ritual nature of the *Nāṭya,* we shall go over to an attempt to reconstrue the historical and cultural situation which predetermined the rise of the Sanskrit drama—an issue closely connected with the origin of the ritual and mythological system which took shape on the *pūjā* basis, and the genesis of the rite proper, which the *Nāṭyaśāstra* singles out as essential for the Indian theatre in its initial stage. The treatise does not allow us to see just what determined the formation of a new ritual archetype, so different from the Vedic ritualism, and brought to life myths unknown to the Vedic tradition. Again, only a broader historical and cultural context can help us to answer these questions: when and in what connection the *pūjā* spread in the Āryan milieu, and what part was played in this process by the scenic tradition and rites which accompanied ancient mysterial dramas. In some instances, answers can be only hypothetical and based on attempted interpretations of the scanty and historically scattered fragments of information, which may at first sight seem totally unconnected with each other. However, the analysis of the *Nāṭyaśāstra* which we have made throws a new light on these facts, allowing us to see them as mosaic figments of a once whole picture, which gives us an idea of a ritualistic culture, parent of the phenomenon known as the Sanskrit drama.

THE *PŪJĀ*. THE GENESIS OF A RITE

Of all the range of problems under review, we shall start

with the origin of the *pūjā*—one of the most complicated and enigmatic issues for Indologists. Many scholars adhere to the hypothesis of its Vedic source. Proceeding from objectively existent similarities in a number of details, they see the *pūjā* as a *yajña* which went through particular transformations. Many general and special studies stress a *yajña-pūjā* succession[74], though the transformation which resulted in a thoroughly different ritual archetype has not received a substantiated explanation to this day. J.A.B.van Buitenen's hypothesis was about the only attempt to explain the matter as he traced the *pūjā* to the *Pravargya*, a Vedic rite preceding the *soma* sacrifice[75]. However, he proceeded solely from external ritual aspects, so his concept failed to win broad recognition[76].

A comparison between the *yajña* and the *pūjā* allows us to assume that formal progress crowned by the *Āgamic* ritual system was hardly possible in Vedic rites. The *pūjā* as a specific practical form of cult rather denies than follows the *yajña*. Apart from the above-cited purely ritualistic arguments, another factor speaks against the *pūjā* as a transformed *yajña*—if this transformation had really taken place, it could do so only very early, at the time when the oldest *maṅḍalas* of the *Ṛgveda* were emerging. The *Ṛgveda* never uses the verb *"pūj"*, semantically connected with the rite and meaning 'revere' or 'glorify', but the root *"pūj"* occurs once in the proper name Śācipūjana (*ṚV*.VIII.17.12) coming up in a verse addressed to Indra, most probably, as one of the epithets going with the god's name. *"Śācipūjana pūjyate' neneti pūjanaṁ stotrādi prakhyāta-pūjana"* (O Śācipūjana, with this word is the *pūjā* [worship] performed—such is the *pūjā* [worship] that starts with a praise), Sāyaṅa comments on this fragment. The *Ṛgveda* commentator turns to a broader context as he explains this invocation of the god, pointing out the use of this name in a particular rite known as the *pūjā*. This allows us to assume that the name Śācipūjana conceals an allusion to the rite, and thus prove its existence at the time when this hymn appeared. The occurrence of the root *"pūj"* is no less scanty in other Vedic texts—several times in the *Āśvalāyana-* and *Śāṅkhyāyana-Gṛhyasūtras* and once in the *Chandogya-Upaniṣad* (*ChUp*.I.II.I)[77]. Be this as it may, this scattered evidence allows us to assume that the *pūjā* and the *yajña* simultaneously coexisted in the Vedic era, the former leading, and the latter as no more than a marginal rite, judging by its rare mentions.

The early 20th century advanced a hypothesis on the Dravidian origin of the *pūjā*. It appeared in numerous studies to receive the most consistent treatment in J.N. Farquhar's article[78]. This, however, was also a mere assumption, rather appealing to the reader's common sense than giving sound proof of non-Āryan origins of the *pūjā*. Even with its appearance, the hypothesis remained plausible but unsubstantiated.

The level attained by the studies of this issue today allows us to turn back to the hypothesis of the Dravidian origin of the *pūjā*. Nothing provides more noteworthy and precise information about the non-Āryan genesis of the rite than the etymology of the term. If the *pūjā* were from the start an Āryan rite, its name would naturally belong to Sanskrit, with highly probable parallels in Indo-European languages. However, the root *"pūj"* was proved as non-existent in any language of this family outside India, and repeated attempts to find its Indo-European background[79] every time demanded provisos and ratiocinations on the word *pūjā* being an isolated summit and a unique linguistic phenomenon without direct analogies in Sanskrit and other Indo-European languages[80]. The absence of Indo-European parallels and the linguistic characteristics of the root conditioned Dravidian etymologies of the term. M. Collins proposed to see the word *pūjā* as a Dravidian borrowing derived from *"pū"*, 'flower', and the root *"ge"*, 'make', represented as *"cey"* in Tamil, *"ge"* in Kannada and *"ce"* in Telugu[81]. This interpretation went well with the ritual symbolism of the *pūjā* as flower sacrifice. J. Charpentier, who also analysed the term in a Dravidic context, conjectured its derivation from the root *"pūsu"*, 'anoint'[82]. He saw the part played in the *pūjā* by red sandal ointment as practical proof of this etymology. Another hypothesis of the Dravidian origin of the term traces it to the root *"pōṭṭu"* or *"pōṟṟu"*, 'revere', 'glorify'[83]. The problem proved complicated enough to give rise to another assumption, of the mixed Dravidian-Indo-European origin of the word. However, diversified these expert opinions may be, the Dravidic etymologies used by M. Mayrhofer in his authoritative etymological dictionary to explain the term *pūjā* remain the most plausible for today[84].

The non-Vedic origin of the flower rite itself is indirectly proved by utter indifference to the *pūjā* displayed in *Brāhmaṇa* ritual texts, which describe the Vedic ritualism down to the least detail. The Dravidian background of this worship form is confirmed by structural representations of an archaic proto-Dravidian rite unearthed in Mohenjo-Daro excavations and identified by R.N. Dankedar as worship of the *pūjā* type[85].

As we see it, the sum total of the available ritual, historical and linguistic information testifies to the non-Aryan origin of the *pūjā*. If we assume it as an intrinsic Dravidian rite, we have to take up another, more general problem of interrelations between the religion of the Vedic era, with the *yajña* as its pivotal rite, and the Hindu religious system centered round the *pūjā*. Indological literature abstains from clearly formulating its predominant viewpoint on the extent to which the Hindu rites and world view differed from Brahmanism, chronologically its immediate predecessor. Even though the impact of the non-Aryan substratum on the formation of Hinduism was stressed more than once, the part played by Dravidian influences has not received precise evaluation[86]. If we acknowledge that a non-Aryan rite became the basis of the Hindu ritual-mythological system, largely at the *yajña*'s expense, we have to recognize that these influences were not external but structural and involving the heart of hearts of the ancient Indian ritual culture.

Symptomatically, none of the extant ancient Indian sources offer information to explain this cardinal typological change of ritualism. Not a trace is to be found of the new cult denounced or approved. Nevertheless, the Vedic period of religious history, primarily connected with the *yajña*, was spectacularly bordered off from its new stage, characterized by the appearançe of the *pūjā*. The tradition under review delineated them at the level of terminology, with whatever directly pertained to the orthodox variety of the Vedic-Brahmanic religion known as *Nigama*—a synonym of the Vedas—while the reformed ritualistic system derived from the *pūjā* became known as the *Āgama* to give the name to a cluster of ritual texts discussed in Chapter I of this work[87].

There was a world of difference between the Vedic liturgical practice and Hindu worship. Vedism and Brahmanism knew no templar edifices, which were obligatory for Hindus. The *yajña*—non-iconic worship of an unseen god—contrasted to the *pūjā* worship of his anthropomorphous hypostases. To put it differently, the Hindu period of religious history saw the *pūjā* mainly as a templar rite of the adoration of a divine image. Both these constituent features of *Āgamic* ritualism are also notable in the ritual-mythological texts of the *Nāṭyaśāstra*.

THE TEMPLAR THEATRE
THE BIRTH OF THE SACRAL ARCHITECTURE

In our analysis of the rites of playhouse foundation and consecration, we noted the pronounced sacral function of the theatre. One question remains open, however: to what an extent did the religious viewpoint spread the polyfunctional nature of the playhouse? Was it a proper temple reqairing regular worship for the well-being of the entire community? Or was it intended for the ritual drama alone?

As we received a description of the playhouse from a treatise on the art of drama, the contemporary mind sees the abode of the *Nāṭya* mainly as a place where dramas are performed—though we can also assume that the traditional mind saw it, above all, as the site of the *pūjā*, without which the drama itself could not exist, losing its point and degrading into a pernicious spectacle. The *Nāṭyaśāstra* expressly points it out: "Without a precious offering of the *pūjā*, we shall not arrange either the stage or the performance" (*NŚ*.1.126).

The results of the *pūjā* went far outside drama sacralisation. They mattered for the whole country and its sovereign. Thus, the description of the theatre foundation points out that a torn measuring cord forebodes political unrest, just as unsteady pillars bring droughts, enemy invasions, deaths and other disasters. A religious ceremony skipped in the theatre meant trouble for the nation and the King, while regular scenic *pūjā* true to the canon guaranteed the King's weal and luck to all men and women, young and old, the city where the theatre was, and the whole country (*NŚ*.3.93-95).

Notably, the numerous prayers of the *Nāṭyaśāstra* rites ask gods for the well-being of the King, Brahmins and the entire community—not only the performance, its sponsors and actors.

On the contrary, the prayers keep them in the background.

There is no proof of the high ritual status of the theatre more graphic than royal participation in its rites. The King appeared on the stage at the decisive moment of the consecration—in an empty playhouse where no dramas had yet been enacted; alone with the priests and priestesses directly involved in the rite. Doubtless, participation in this rite of his consecration and sacralisation of his power was the one and only purpose of his coming. His sheer presence in the playhouse, and the purely ritual aim of his appearance show how important the sacral theatre was for ancient Indian religious life.

All this allows us to assume with a great degree of certainty that the playhouse originally had a templar status and manifold sacral functions centered round the *pūjā* and ritual drama. To this day, we do not know a single extant playhouse—hence the doubt of whether the theatre construction practice existed at all[88]. Nevertheless, we dare to ascribe their current absence to other reasons. Proceeding from contemporary ideas, archeologists sought theatre buildings of a pronounced secular character, entirely designed for theatricals, while they ought to look for templar edifices, mainly serving the *pūjā* and only then, the mystery drama.

Chapter II of the *Nāṭyaśāstra* bears out this assumption. Even its superficial reading draws us to the conclusion that the treatise means not conventionalised, conjectural to an extent, ideas of the playhouse but existent buildings. It mentions three kinds of such regular buildings—square, rectangular and triangular, each with the maximum, average and minimum dimensions specified. Respectively, the sides were to be 32, 44 or 108 cubits long. According to the treatise, Bharata owed his knowledge of proportions to none other than Viśvakarman, which seemingly implies that all playhouses of these sizes were holy to an equal extent. However, as it is, the treatise prescribes only rectangular structures, no longer than 64 cubits (over 29 metres) and no wider than 32 (over 15 metres). To all appearances, the time before the *Nāṭyaśāstra* appeared knew just such rectangular edifices for the *pūjā* and the *Nāṭya*, with an impressive floor area of over 400 square metres. As we know from the treatise, the majority of theatres had two storeys and small windows. All their parts were of brick or stone, with wooden pillars and stage. After the construction was finished, the building was decorated with the wall surface smoothed out, plastered, whitewashed and painted with murals representing genre scenes and decorative patterns. The *Nāṭyaśāstra* prescribes climbing plants, and men and women in erotic play—at first sight, a preposterous metier for a house of prayer. Don't let us forget, however, that the Indian tradition viewed carnal love as a manifestation of divinity, and so erotic paintings and sculptures were widespread in temple decoration.

After the theatre was painted, numerous wooden statues were placed in it (*NŚ*.2.76). Simultaneously, the pillars were adored with *Śālabhañjikā* sculptural compositions (representations of a woman and a tree) extremely widespread in Indian art.

The *Nāṭyaśāstra* precepts on theatre construction resemble architectural treatises (*Śilpa Śāstras*) and chapters of the *Āgamic* treatises fixing the rules of Hindu templar architecture[89]. Their comparison with Chapter II of the *Nāṭyaśāstra* allows us to precisely state the name and type of the templar structure used for the ritual drama. According to the treatise, the theatre resembled a mountain cave; hence its name *Guhā* (lit., cave) (*NŚ*.2.80). We know *Guhā* temples from ancient Indian architectural treatises, which paid them ample attention and mentioned them as one of the two basic types of the early Hindu temple[90]. The playhouse temple and *Guhā* temple were the same thing—suffice it to compare the size of the theatre, according to the *Nāṭyaśāstra*, with the *Guhā* characteristics. Both were based on a 16 cubit module. The *Guhā*, like the playhouse, was a rectangular one-room structure with the length twice the width. Such temples were of brick and usually one-storeyed. There was, however, a two-storey variety. All this draws us to a vital conclusion that any *Guhā* temple, of the kind we know from archeological finds, could serve as playhouse.

Thus, playhouses as a variety of temples were, doubtless, present in the Indian past. More than that, the *Nāṭyaśāstra* allows us to assume that the templar *pūjā* practice with the accompanying *Nāṭya* emerged in the earliest days of sacral architecture. First, this is borne out by the *Nāṭyaśāstra* legend which says that Viśvakarman built the first playhouse soon after the first drama was performed. Then, the fact that the *Sūtradhāra* (lit., holder of the cord), architect or master-builder, was the central figure of the *Pūrvaraṅga,* and leader of the performing company—kind of leading performer—reveals that the drama and templar construction were closely linked from the start. We can also assume that the terms for the templar builder, the chief priest in the *Pūrvaraṅga* and the leading performer in the drama do not coincide by chance but reflect the period in the evolving tradition when the sacral functions of theatre construction, the *pūjā* offered in the theatre, and its ritual performances all belonged to one person, the *Sūtradhāra.* The term for his scenic assistant, *Sthāpaka* (lit., builder) is also telling. Later, as the ritual knowledge extended and grew more sophisticated, ritual duties naturally had to be shared out. The no longer clear coincidence of the terms for 'actors' and 'builders' was the only remnant from the archaic time, and moved scholars to many hypotheses[91].

We shall sum up the above by assuming that ancient India knew a unique type of temple of the *Guhā* variety—sites of regular *pūjā,* with their universal sacral message, and ritual dramas. There is another reason why these houses have not been unearthed to this day—the contemporary mind has quite different ideas. Most probably, the *Nāṭya* house was not so much the theatre with plays preceded by sacred rites, on an obligatory basis or not, as a unique temple for rites in the drama form, which, like the European liturgical drama, complemented the obligatory canonical liturgy.

Importantly, the idea of the temple-theatre long outlived the early ritual *Nāṭya* in Indian culture. As we see it, the medieval *Naṭmandiras* (playhouses or dancing halls) within templar ensembles were later interpretations of the same idea. They served for ritual dancing, and some kinds of the *pūjā* performed to great congregations on religious feasts[92]. The vast numbers of *Apsara* and *Gandharva* sculptures on the facades of Hindu temples testify to this unity of the theatre and the worship as they stand in postures prescribed by the *Nāṭyaśāstra.*

THE HOLY IMAGE
THE APPEARANCE OF AN ICONIC CULT

The ritual and mythological information of the *Nāṭyaśāstra* gives us an idea of the *pūjā* as adoration of a holy image. The treatise does not devote a special chapter to descriptions of such images or the techniques of their making. However, as we said above, *Śālabhañjikā* sculptures, which were outside direct objects of adoration, decorated playhouse pillars, playing an essential ritual role and creating the impression of celestial maidens' actual presence.

The description of theatre consecration rite also provides information about worshipped holy images. The priest who sacralized the stage started with "installing the deities on it"—probably, both wooden or stone statues and actual gods, present as substances ideal and unseen. Oblique allusions in the *Nāṭyaśāstra* allow us this conjecture. First among these invisible presences were deities of the lower pantheon, to whom the treatise alludes only in the plural. Most of them belonged to the retinue of a god, and were invoked to the stage in huge numbers as, for instance, the *Bhūta* hosts who accompanied Śiva.

The characteristics of supreme deities, on the contrary, presuppose actual sculptures, in particular, "Brahmā seated on a lotus" in a posture which clearly points at the widespread Indian iconography of the god who, according to tradition, was born of a lotus flower. To all appearances, all the other gods mentioned in the treatise were also represented by ritual statuary. If so, the *Nāṭyaśāstra* precepts demand from the priest an arrangement of the statues of Śiva, Viṣṇu Nārāyaṇa, Indra, Skanda, Sarasvatī, Lakṣmī, *Agni,* Yama, Mitra and other gods round Brahmā, in eight sectors oriented on and between the cardinal points.

There are many arguments to bear out this assumption. Thus, when the *Nāṭyaśāstra* sums up the rules for placing gods in the *maṇḍala,* it stresses that "in accordance with the rules all the deities are to be installed in their [proper] forms and colours" (*NŚ*.3.32). This is possible only if material sculptural images are meant—the most impressive of all possible visual representations of visible beings—with shape and colour as their most salient features. The stage arrangement of the gods is also telling as it precisely follows the Hindu templar arrangement of sacral statuary. The image of the god to whom the temple was consecrated was the first to take its place, in the centre of the edifice. Next, sculptures of other gods were placed to its four sides, oriented on the cardinal points. The ceremony ended with equal intervals measured out to arrange other holy images midway between the cardinal points[93].

This allows us to assume with a great degree of certainty that scenic ritualism knew divine images as objects of worship. Thus, the *Nāṭyaśāstra*, as the *Āgamic* treatises, records a syncretic cult which demanded not only the worship of an unseen god materialised only in worshippers' imagination but ritual adoration of his physical form open to visual perception. Probably, the affinity of image worship and the theatre is much more essential and profound than believed hitherto. The emergence of ritual images of gods received no special treatment from Indologists. We don't know when, how and in what ritual context the anthropomorphous canon appeared in Hinduism. A more particular question also remains unanswered: was the *pūjā* an iconic worship form from the start, and if it wasn't, what promoted the emergence of the iconic cult?

We see the emergence of individual features in the anthropomorphous imagery of a particular deity as following from ritual drama performances, with gods, demons and other supernatural beings for the only heroes. Doubtless, the scenic action made them differ from each other in appearance, which was possible only if each had a permanent set of individual features to be represented by the costume, make-up and hairdo.

This anthropomorphous canon could emerge only in two ways: either the performers of the rite borrowed the iconographic types of the Hindu pantheon—we don't know where—and put life in them by making them *Nāṭya* characters, or they gradually gave material shape to the basic ideas of gods' appearance as they were to enact myths and had no etalon to proceed from.

We can't flatly deny the first variant, having to admit, however, that the facts we know for today rather refute than support it. As we pointed out above, Vedic ritualism had no anthropomorphous images of gods. At any rate, even if they existed, they did not play any part in this practical ritualism and appeared only rather late, in the post-Vedic period of ancient Indian ritual culture. We can say this for certain if we proceed from the texts of the *Brāhmaṇas*. Thus, ritual statues of gods, unknown in the Vedic era, were by no means part and parcel of the *yajña* cult. By this alone, the *pūjā* could not inherit them from the Vedic ritual system. Possibly, they could be borrowed from Dravidian tribes together with the *pūjā*. But then, we don't know anything about this form of Dravidian piety and, even if we take this unsubstantiated statement for granted, it gives us no explanation why and how the anthropomorphous imagery of Vedic gods—Brahmā, Indra, *Agni*, Mitra, *Yama* and others—emerged in the aboriginal cults even before Āryans adopted the *pūjā*.

On the other hand, make-up, costumes and other expressive means known in the stage world sufficed to create highly individualised and at the same time conventional image of any deity. As the *Nāṭyaśāstra* points out, the outward appearance of dramatis personae was determined by a combination of various *abhinayas*, ways of scenic representation, embodied in the *Āṅgika abhinaya*—movements and gestures—and the *Āhārya abhinaya*, make-up and costume (*NŚ*.23.2-3). The colour symbolism of the make-up, as described by the treatise, mainly concerns divine personages. Thus, it requires a gold colour scheme for Śiva, Sūrya, Brahmā and Skanda; white for Soma, Indra, Varuṅa and Bṛhaspati; yellow for *Agni*; dark blue for Nārāyaṇa, Nara and Vāsuki; blue for *Yama*, *Daityas*, *Dānavas*, *Rākṣasas*, *Piśācas* and *Guhyakas*, and motley combinations of all colours for *Yakṣas*, *Gandharvas* and *Nāgas* (*NŚ*.23.90-94). The list of jewellry is accompanied by an indication that they shall be worn by the gods and royalty (*NŚ*.23.20). A detailed description of the appearance of goddesses, *Apsaras*, *Yakṣa* and *Nāga* maidens goes together with the description of female characters' make-up and costumes (*NŚ*.23.49-60), while mortal women are to wear their country's attire (*NŚ*.23.62).

The actors varied their movement to present their characters' state of mind. They used scenic step of many kinds, static attitudes, and a conventional gesticular idiom. As we see it, scenic movement combined with make-up and costumes made the basis of anthropomorphous divine images as scenic likenesses of gods received a wealth of easily recognisable iconographic characteristics. It was easy to go over from scenic images, with their fixed costumes, hairdos and colouring, to more lasting likenesses—statues.

This assumption is borne out by doubtless closeness of the *abhinaya* techniques which helped the actors to feel as if really transformed into their characters, and artistic techniques employed to create pictorial and sculptural representations of gods[94]. As is commonly recognized, the colour scheme in ancient Indian art was thoroughly conventionalised and governed by the patterns of scenic make-up which evolved in the long progress of the theatre. Artists also owed the lines and shades of colour which produced the three-dimensional effect to patterns in which actors' bodies were toned. More than that, they were known by the *Nāṭyaśāstra* term *vartana*, body make-up[95].

Sculptures of Hindu gods on temple facades have poses described in the *Nāṭyaśāstra*. Statues and relief figures are represented with gestures from the scenic gesticular idiom, enabling experts up to this day to illustrate the theoretical precepts of the treatise with actual figures from templar decoration.

Thus, paintings and sculptures of gods, most probably, received their attire, make-up and postures from actors who played gods. Instead of imitating iconographies from static images which appeared out of the blue no one knows when, the stage, with its sophisticated tradition of enacting Hindu myths, produced sets of divine features later fixed in paintings and statuary.

There is no reason to think that Aryans borrowed a whole religious system from Dravidians—a cult whose constituent features included templar construction and liturgical imagery. Such a cult, most probably, never existed at all—but the existence of the *pūjā* was doubtless, ousted by the *yajña*, as it was, to the margins of ritual and public life. It would be more correct to assume that only an idea or, at most, the basic pattern of flower sacrifice was borrowed. With its developed symbolical semantics, this pattern gradually gave rise to sophisticated ceremonial rites which we know from the *Nāṭyaśāstra* and the *Āgamas*. As the holy communion in Christian ritualism demands a firmly arranged sequence of liturgical actions, so was the *pūjā*—part of ritual offering—framed on logically interlinked sacral events. A wealth of particular rites arose on the basis of one widely varied archetype to pursue different ritual goals, but all shared the generic name of *pūjā*.

As our comparison of the *Āgamic* and scenic rites demonstrated, the *pūjā* partly received its elements from the Vedic ritualism. Others, most probably, arose from independent efforts of pious creativity—especially the singing, music, dancing, its specific movements, conventional poses and precise iconic gestures which were the symbolical bases of the sacred rite, rather than decorations of the *pūjā*. Unknown in the Vedic ritualism, all these innovations have a pronounced scenic nature. As we see it, nothing but a long parallel evolution of the rite and the ritual drama could make the sacral techniques of the *pūjā* so close to scenic expressive means. In the final analysis, this evolution conditioned the appearance of anthropomorphous images of gods as repeating the symbolism of actors' costumes, movement and make-up. The coherent performance of the flower sacrifice and the scenic myth alone can explain why the playhouse known from the *Nāṭyaśāstra* was at the same time referred to as the first temple for *pūjā* offerings in the legend.

Proceeding from the above, we can assume the following sequence of the formative stages of the iconic cult. At first, gods acted in the flesh only in the ritual drama, which had particular techniques to represent them. Step by step, these techniques grew to be treated as a way to communicate with the suprapersonal world. So they found their way to the rites connected with drama performances, and later into the *Āgamic* forms of the *pūjā*. Characteristically, self-identification with a divine being through conventional poses and gestures not merely became an *Āgamic* sacred practice but survived to this day in the many forms of Hindu ritualism. Evidently, the *pūjā* could not acquire the first cult imagery before the stage gave final shape to the anthropomorphous likenesses of the Hindu pantheon. The three kinds of divine incarnation—through the actor in the drama, through the priest performing the *pūjā*, and through the sculptor as he worked with stone, wood or metal—share a symbolism and appeal to one system of ritual ideas.

Importantly, the adoration of a sacred image or symbol fully agreed with the pivotal dogmatic idea of the *pūjā*—worship by laying offerings at the foot of the contemplated holy image, not with the help of flames consuming a sacrifice. Most probably, at first this idea determined the unique sacral status of many ritual objects involved in the *pūjā* and considered abodes of deities, and at a certain stage, an extensive use of ritual statuary. When a god was considered ideally present with the congregation, it was supposed mentally to reconstrue his appearance by recalling numerous specific details whose sum total was not unlike an iconographic cyclopedia with references to his sculptures or paintings seen many times before.

THE *NĀṬYAŚĀSTRA* AS A PHENOMENON OF EARLY HINDU CULTURE

Thus, we have demonstrated that the essential features of ritual specifics of the *Āgamic pūjā* have direct analogies in the *Nāṭyaśāstra*. More than that, this study shows a close link between templar construction and the emergence of holy images, on the one hand, and the appearance of the scenic *pūjā* and stage versions of epic myths. As we ought to stress in this connection, the *Āgama*s know the tradition of templar worship of gods' images in a well-developed and finally established form. Doubtless, the *Āgama*s make us think of a widespread and flourishing religious culture, whereas the *Nāṭyaśāstra*, as we see it, reflects a much earlier period of its existence, fixing not a final and indisputable canon but rather the many stages of religious creativity as a living process. The fact that the treatise, which appeared in the early centuries A.D., offers us probably the first detailed description of the *pūjā* does not in the slightest contradict this assumption, which arose on the basis of studies of particular worship forms. *Āgamic* treatises, little studied as they are, have very approximate datings[96]. They are assumed to have appeared at about the same time as a group, while the corpus of manuscripts comprising the basic and supplementary *Upāgamas* had taken its final shape by the 9th century A.D. to reflect medieval Hinduism[97]. Supposedly, they were preceded by older ritual texts which corresponded to the initial formative stage of Hinduism—a proto-*Āgama*, which has not gone down to us. Thus, the *Nāṭyaśāstra* turns out to be much older than all the *Āgamic* literature available today. It fixes many features of the emergence of the iconic cult and, at the same time, is the earliest source on the *pūjā* ritualism. As we feel bound to remind in this connection, the ritual texts of the *Nāṭyaśāstra* took shape much earlier than the conventionally accepted 1st and 2nd centuries.

It is appropriate here to pose the question when templar rites of image worship became spread. The *Āgamic* treatises give documentary proof that confessionally varied iconic cults flourished in medieval India. Proceeding from the dating of the *Nāṭyaśāstra,* we can assume with a great degree of certainty that sophisticated forms of templar ritualism connected with stage performances existed as early as the turn of the present millennium.

Analyses of earlier literary sources with consideration for the conventionality present in the datings of the majority of ancient Indian manuscripts allow us to see that the earliest testimony to the existence of an iconic cult goes back to the mid-1st millennium B.C. Thus, Pāṅini's grammar, the *Aṣṭādhyāyī,* dated 5th to 4th century B.C., mentions images of gods, to which it refers as *Pratikṛti (Pāṇ.*5.3.96) or, more specially, *Ārca (Pāṇ.*5.2.101). As he regards the rule for adding suffixes to divine names, such as Śiva and Skanda, Pāṇini makes a passing mention of statues of gods and a specific activity connected with serving holy images, which gives decent earnings (*Pāṇ.*5.3.99). The *Aṣṭādhyāyī* gives enough information to conclude that in the mid-1st millenium B.C., *pūjā* worship was widespread in India alongside the Vedic *yajña.* We come across repeated references to the *pūjā* in Pāṇini's grammar (*Pāṇ.*3.3.105; 8.1.67).

The *pūjā* as iconic worship was known to the ancient commentators of the *Aṣṭādhyāyī.* We find allusions to it in Kāṭyāyana's Commentary on the *Sūtras,* written a century or two after Pāṇini (*Vārt.*1.3.25; *Pat.,* vol.I, p.281), and in Patañjali, presumable author of the *Mahābhāṣya* (2nd century B.C.), who refers to the *pūjā* as a widespread and topical ritual practice. He mentions the Mauryas, who encouraged the making of statues, earlier used only as objects of worship, to enrich their treasury with gold (*Pat.,* vol.II, p.429).

This information allows us to date the emergence of the iconic cult to the mid-1st millennium B.C. The first cult buildings must have appeared a bit later. They are mentioned by Pāṇini's commentators (*Pat*., vol.I, p.436). Scattered references to temples (*Devatāyatana)*, abodes of the gods (*Devakula*) and holy images (*Devatārca*) are met in the *Mānava, Baudhāyana* and *Śāṅkhyāyana Gṛhyasūtras*, and in the *Gautama* and *Apastamba Dharmasūtras*, which the authoritative P.V. Kane dates to the 5th or 4th century B.C.[98] The earlier parts of *Mahābhārata*, which presumably appeared at the same time, also mention holy images and temples. All this fragmentary evidence, preserved often by chance in sources devoted to other themes, perfectly agrees with archeological data. The earliest extant ruins of stone temples and samples of stone statuary, going back to the 4th and 3rd centuries B.C.[99], show an established canon and the exquisite craftsmanship of stonemasons and sculptors, which had acquired refinement, as experts think, in the period of wooden architecture preceding stone sculpture and building. Thus, the tradition of templar architecture and decorative sculpture must have emerged several centuries earlier, at the same conventionalised borderline of the mid-1st millennium B.C.

According to the *Aṣṭādhyāyī*, that same period was noted for the formation of religious and mythological ideas linked to the ritual practice of image worship. Pāṇini refers to Śiva and Skanda among the post-Vedic deities whom, as Pataṭjali noted, "the Vedas do not intend together for offering gifts" (*Pāṇ*.6.3.26; *Pat*., vol.III, p.149). Pāṇini mentions Bhavānī, Rudrānī, Śarvānī and Mṛdānī—names corresponding to the female hypostasis of Śiva and derived from his four names (*Pāṇ*.4.1.59). The ancient grammarian also points out the adoration of *Mahārāja*, or Vessavana-Kubera—the lord of the four keepers of the cardinal points, who may be identified with the *Lokapālas*, unknown in the Vedic tradition but important in the mythology of the *Nāṭyaśāstra* and the medieval *Āgamic* texts (*Pāṇ*.4.4.135). More evidence to non-Vedic worship forms and related religious-mythological ideas being widespread in the mid-1st millenium B.C. is provided by the tradition which says that Pāṇini received the initial and essential *Sūtras* of the *Aṣṭādhyāyī* from Śiva and thus makes us see the grammarian as a supporter, or at least witness, of non-Vedic religious ideas.

The early *Gṛhyasūtras*, which appeared at about the same time, describe a rite known as *Śūlagava*, where Rudra-Śiva is worshipped as supreme god. The *Āśvalāyana Gṛhyasūtra*, dated no later than the 4th century B.C., mentions twelve names of Rudra, adding that he owns all names in the world (*AśvGṛSū*.IV.9.17; 27-29).

When we regarded *pūjā* ritualism, we advanced a hypothesis of ancient *Nāṭya* performances as closely connected with the emergence of holy images and, in the final analysis, of the iconic cult. However, it would be historically plausible only if the scenic tradition already existed in the mid-1st millennium B.C. The *Aṣṭādhyāyī*, among others, provides proof that the theatre did exist and even had a theoretical background at the time. Many scholars pointed out Pāṇini's references to *Naṭasūtras*, which go together with the epithet 'enigmatic' in the common practice. Many books have been written to discuss whether these *Sūtras* were manuals for dancers and mimes, or for proper actors[100].

The doubt whether the term *Naṭa* ought to be translated as actor was based on the conviction that the theatre had not yet emerged as a whole by the mid-1st millennium B.C., and only parts of the future unity—dancing, music and pantomime—were in existence. The *Aṣṭādhyāyī* makes us think, however, that this assumption is wrong: Pāṇini already knew the difference between *Nṛtta*, dancing (*Pāṇ*.3.1.145) and *Nāṭya*, drama proper (*Pāṇ*.4.3.129). Of importance are his observations on the linguistic connection between these terms. As the *Aṣṭādhyāyī* specifies, *Nāṭya*, not *Nṛtta*, was derived from *Naṭa*. Probably, these kinds of scenic action were mutually separated not only terminologically but in practice. In particular, Patañjali's comments on the corresponding *Sūtras* by Pāṇini make a special proviso for the use of the term *Nṛtta* to denote dancing. The *Nāṭyaśāstra*, which, doubtless, concerns well-developed forms of the drama, repeatedly refers to actors as *Naṭas*. Proceeding from this, we can say that even in Pāṇini's time, the term *Naṭa* denoted not only dancers—or dancers least of all—but actors in the proper sense of this word, and by *Nāṭya*, meant a performance close to the drama typologically and according to the nature of its imagery. The *Aṣṭādhyāyī* provides the answer, to an extent, to the question whether the *Naṭasūtras* and the practice they described had secular or sacral functions. Pāṇini mentions these *Sūtras* in the section which enumerates treatises written in the various Vedic schools. He cites the *Naṭasūtras* of Śilālin and Kṛśaśva with the *Brāhmaṇas, Kalpasūtras* and *Śrautasūtras,* referring to them as sacral writings. In his comment to Pāṇini, Pantañjali points out that the study of the *Naṭasūtras* differed from the accepted textual form of passing ritual lore on, as it took place on the stage: "The teaching [starts] when the beginners appear on the stage [and say]: 'Let us listen to [and learn from] the *Naṭa*" (*Pāṇ*.1.4.29; Pat., vol.I, p.329). Pāṇini's commentators attributed the *Naṭasūtras* to the *Āmnāya* tradition—a fact of the utmost importance[101]. By *Āmnāya* were meant sacred legends and writ, so it belonged to the tradition to which the medieval *Āgamic* texts ascribed themselves, when the system of ideas fixed there was meant by *Āmnāya*. Thus, we can assume that Pāṇini's time saw *Naṭasūtras* as religious works connected with a kind of ritual practice.

If we are to specify this practice, we must regard the succession from the *Naṭasūtras* to the text of the *Nāṭyaśāstra* known to us. There is an opinion that the treatise was directly preceded by the *Naṭasūtra* by Śilālin[102], mentioned in the *Śatapatha Brāhmaṇa* as master of rites (*ŚBr*.XIII.5.3.3). As follows from Patañjali's comment, the *Aṣṭādhyāyī* meant the name of a school ascending to renowned Śilālin, rather than the particular author of a *Sūtra*. A reference to this school as really existent is found in the *Ānupada Sūtra* (*ĀnSū*.VI.5). As the Indian tradition had it, schools gave their names to books written in them, for instance, the *Śailālika Brāhmaṇa*, which has not gone down to us but is mentioned in the *Apastamba Śrauta Sūtra* (*AŚtrSū*.VI.4.7). Notably, the *Nāṭyaśāstra* often refers to drama performers as *Śailālakās*—a term evidently derived from Śailālinas, a term which, according to Pāṇini's precept (*Pāṇ*.4.2.66), designated Śilālin school students of *Naṭasūtras*. This is a weighty testimony of the link between Śilālin's *Naṭasūtra* and the *Nāṭyaśāstra*. No doubt, the Śilālin school was prominent in the progress of the theatre. It was not for nothing that the ancient Indian tradition knew actors as the *Śailūṣa*.

Thus we can state that *Naṭasūtras*—testimony to a theoretical appraisal of the theatre—appeared in the mid-1st millennium B.C., at the time when *pūjā* worship spread in India and gave rise to related mythological ideas. It was an era when the theatre evolved within ritual practices. The link between Śilālin's *Naṭasūtra* and the *Nāṭyaśāstra*, and the religious nature of the *Naṭasūtras*, within the *Āmnāya* tradition, make us think that these lost treatises were, in fact, ritual texts describing scenic rites of the *pūjā* type and the accompanying mystery plays. This assumption allows us to see ritual-mythological information of the *Nāṭyaśāstra* as the earliest traces of an ideology which disseminated the *pūjā* among Āryans. Let us turn again to the Genesis myth as reflected in the legend of the creation of the theatre. As we see it, this legend mythologically substantiates actual historical events, so we cite its relevant part in much detail. The legend opens with Sages asking Bharata, the legendary author of the *Nāṭyaśāstra*: " 'This *Nāṭyaveda* which thou hath composed the due way, and which is similar to the Vedas, how did originate, O Brahmin, and what for?' Hearing these words of the Sages, Bharata spake thus in reply about the *Nāṭyaveda*: 'Let the origin of the *Nāṭyaveda* devised by Brahmā be heard by you. O Brahmins, in the days of yore when the Golden Age (*Kṛtayuga*) of [Manu] Svayambhuva passed and the Silver Age (*Tretāyuga*) of Many Vaivasvata arrived, the people became victims of lust and covetousness and were engaged in rustic rites, overwhelmed by jealousy and deluded by wrath, wavering between happiness and misery. Then great Indra with other leading gods submitted to Pitāmaha (Brahmā): 'We wish to have an entertainment that would deserve being visible and audible. The Vedic discussion and practice cannot be proclaimed among those born as Śūdra castes. Be pleased to create another, fifth Veda, common to all the *Varṇas*'. 'Let it be so', said he in reply and then, having dismissed the King of gods (Indra), he resorted to yoga power and recalled to mind the four Vedas. He then thought: 'I shall make a fifth Veda, entitled *Nāṭya* with *Itihāsa*. It shall conduce to duty (*dharma*), wealth (*artha*) as well as fame, shall contain good counsel and a collection of didactic maxims; it shall give guidance to the future people in all their actions, will be enriched by the teaching of all *Śāstras* and demonstrate all types of arts and crafts. *Nāṭya* will be its name' Fully recalling to his mind all the Vedas after this resolution, the Holy Lord created *Nāṭyaveda*, born out of the four Vedas. Thus was created the graceful *Nāṭyaveda*, having its origin in and connection with the main Vedas and supplementary Upavedas by the holy Brahmā, who is omniscient. After evolving the *Nāṭyaveda* Brahmā said to Indra: 'Myths and legends (*Itihāsa*) have been composed by me, put it to practical use among the gods. May this *Nāṭyaveda* be passed on to those among them who are skilful, learned, bold in speech and indefatigable'. On hearing what has been mentioned by Brahmā, Indra bowed to him with folded palms and replied thus: 'O the best and holy One, the gods are unworthy of the art of *Nāṭya* because they are incapable of receiving, retaining, comprehending and putting it into practice. The Sages, who possess the esoteric mystery of the Vedas and are firm in the observance of holy vows, are capable of receiving, retaining and putting it into practice' " (*NŚ*.1.5-23). After this, wise Bharata taught the art of *Nāṭya* to his hundred sons "on Brahmā's order and in the desire of weal for people" (*NŚ*.1.40).

Abstracting from the mythological form of this legend, we notice the following essential features. The legend presents the *Nāṭyaveda* as new sacral knowledge directly linked to the Vedas—even comprising their parts. This is very important, as not only the treatise on the theatre but most of the *Āgamic* manuscripts recognise the Vedas as an infallible religious writ and their sources[103]. Even though the *Āgamic* ideology spectacularly reappraised the role and importance of the Vedas, making them no more than revelations of the god considered supreme in this or that confession, the very fact that they were part of the sacred canon clearly shows the desire to emphasize succession of the *Āgamic* tradition to the heritage of the Vedic era—a succession far beyond mere declaration. This is demonstrated the most graphically by Vedic ritual traits in the rites of the *Nāṭyaśāstra* and the *Āgamas*. As we showed while comparing particular rites, the Vedic *Homa* libation—a variety of the *Haviryajña*—became part and parcel of the *pūjā*. This book does not regard home worship forms of the *Pākayajña* type. We feel obliged to notice, however, that they, too, retained full validity in Hinduism, which accepted them without the slightest change. Characteristically, of the three basic types of Vedic worship the system of the *pūjā* adopted the rites that were only in the background of the hierarchy of the *Brāhmaṇa* texts and secondary in the religious system of the *yajña,* whereas the *soma* offering—the heart of Vedic ritualism—went into oblivion, though some aspects of the *Soma* cult received a mythological reappraisal to start a new life in the myth of *Amṛtamanthana.*

The legend under review says that the sacred knowledge of the *Nāṭyaveda,* invention of the supreme Hindu god, was passed unto the Brahmins to know and use. Since then, they have been performing the *Nāṭya* and the *pūjā* preceding it. We can't see it as a casual remark but a reflection of historical reality, which makes us assume that the *pūjā* was adapted in the Brahmin milieu. According to the legend, Brahmins had acquired the esoteric Vedic knowledge—i.e., had gone through special schooling required to qualify as full members of the priestly *varṇa*—before they received the *Nāṭya* doctrine. This mention is fully in keeping with the fact that *Naṭasūtra*s emerged in Vedic schools, centres of *Brāhmaṇa* learning. At the same time, it explains why later only Brahmins qualified for templar priesthood. As we have to point out here, the status of the templar priest, passed from father to son for centuries, was anything but elevated in the Middle Ages, the peak of Hinduism. The majority of templar priests were offspring of Brahmin families of fairly low birth—the Brahmins whom the past left outside the priestly elite, performers of solemn *Śrauta* rites in the Vedic era. This drives us to the conclusion that the Dravidian *pūjā* was borrowed by the lower Brahmin strata, which took no part in the opulent *Śrauta* rites, centered round *soma* libations. This fact alone made them the least interested in its preservation. At the same time, they were far more devoted to ritualism and the idea of regular rites than other *varṇa*s. We see it as the decisive motive for the adaptation and dissemination of the non-Āryan *pūjā*. In their desire to affirm a new kind of sacrifice, these Brahmins spared no effort to bring out their links with the Vedic tradition to which they originally belonged[104].

This legend of the *Nāṭyaśāstra* has another salient feature—

the ritual democratization of the new faith. Unlike the Vedic canon, it opened to all *varṇas*, even the Śūdras. This argument substantiates the necessity for a fifth Veda, to which the entire laity could find an access. In this sense, the sacred knowledge of the *Nāṭyaveda* was counterposed to the Brāhmaṇic theology, with its pivotal dogma of the Āryans' ritually exceptional status and the twiceborn as the select few, who inherited the right to sacrifice *soma*. Judging by the *Āgamas*, the liturgical practice remained open to all in the Middle Ages. Then, too, women, members of the lower *varṇas*, and half-castes took part in the *pūjā*. If we regard *Nāṭyaśāstra* legends as historically authentic information, we can safely assume that the dissemination of the *pūjā* among *Āryans* involved strata barred from many Vedic rites into religious life of the community.

An analysis of this information leads us to the conclusion that the main goal of the *pūjā* was to oust *soma* libations, whose practice died away in the post-Vedic era. Thus, the *pūjā* became entitled to the status of a solemn festive rite performed to large congregations. Probably, this factor accounted from the start for the overall idea of a spectacular, stagy divine worship, encouraged by ornate aesthetics intrinsic to the *pūjā*, for which the natural beauty of flowers and the exquisite aroma of incense were so important. More than that, its theatrical nature, to all appearances, allowed to involve even the least trained worshippers from the lowest *varṇas* as it preached new religious values in the varied and easily understandable idiom of a stage performance.

As we have shown above, the idea of a scenically represented myth merging with the *pūjā* in a single pious ceremony, doubtless, played the central part in this innovation. After the *pūjā* offering, Brahmin reformers went over to their stage performance of a myth—a simple and impressive sermon of the basic religious and mythological dogmas of the new religion. The *Nāṭya* acquainted the congregation with diverse canonical traditions, as represented by *Amṛtamanthana* and *Tripuradāha*—the eventful bases of a stage sermon.

All this explains why none other than a treatise on the theatre reflected the oldest premises of the *Āgamic* ideology, which came to replace the Vedic *Nigama*. Though a part of these facts could be collected in the medieval *Āgamas*, the legend of the *Nāṭyaśāstra*—an exhaustive collection of these facts—gathers this scattered mosaic into a comprehensive picture which, as we see it, characterizes the sources of the post-Vedic Hinduism.

The last and essential question is related to historical events which conditioned the adaptation of a non-Āryan worship form. The legend we have regarded gives a peculiar description of the time when the *Nāṭyaveda* appeared—a time of trouble at the borderline between the Golden and Silver ages; a time when religious precepts were given up and carnal pleasure reigned supreme. More than that, the impious era itself necessitated the emergence of a new Veda. As the legend stresses, Brahmā's work is able to improve the situation in another aspect—as a universal knowledge containing the essence of all sciences and crafts, and able to improve public morals and restore the lost law and order[105]. The actual historical time referred to as the end of the Golden Age was, to all appearances, the mid-1st millennium B.C., with its historical and cultural situation that placed the non-Āryan *pūjā* among the canonical Vedic rites.

We know that time as a watershed of the Indian civilization, an era which shook the seemingly unshakable pillars of the Vedic religion. Brāhmaṇism, with its recently all-embracing precepts of life, ceased to correspond to the new spiritual demands of the community. Its theology was over-complicated, the ramified system of precepts defied practical following, and the cult ceremonies devoid of sufficient impact. Presumably, the fall of the Brāhmaṇic tradition was largely conditioned by the crisis of Vedic ritualism—mainly the solemn *soma* rituals lasting for many days. However, strictly Brāhmaṇic theology might have insisted on their obligatory and regular performance, the social status of the *Śrauta* rites had actually fallen far below these demands.

As we know, the reformative spirit of the time gave rise to many religious trends. One of them, like Buddhism and Jainism, was destined to play a crucial part in Indian culture. Others remained only as a distant, semi-legendary echo in the tradition. They all offered alternative roads for development, and all faced the necessity to reform the Brāhmaṇic ritual system. In particular, Buddhism and Jainism accounted for relatively rare variants of extra-ritual religious movements, which gave up all pageantry in their sacral practices. As we see it, this was a response to the unpopular Vedic ritualism. The doctrine which helped to introduce the non-Āryan *pūjā* into it offered a contrasting way to solve the problem. Possibly, the *pūjā* had a magnetism as a worship form new to the Āryan community—first, as a rite sanctified by its very age and, second, offering an alternative to the *yajña*, which no longer corresponded to the new spiritual values.

The ritual and mythological system which, presumably, arose in the mid-1st millennium B.C. round the non-Āryan *pūjā* was immediate historical predecessor of Hinduism which, in the first century A.D., ousted all other religious trends from India to become its leading religion for a long time. This system was a unique link between the faith of the Vedic era and mature Hinduism, as represented by various confessional trends in the Middle Ages. Awareness of the fact that this ritual-mythological system did exist is the central conclusion made in this book. It remains, however, for the future to comprehensively reconstrue early Hindu culture with its fruit—the drama, the epics, the iconic cult and templar worship.

NOTES

[1] We feel the following works on the *Nāṭyaśāstra* deserving special notice: R. Daumal. *Bharata. L' origin du theatre.* P., 1970; S.K. De. *The Problems of Bharata and Ādi-Bharata.*—S.K. De. *Some Problems of Sanskrit Poetics.* Calcutta, 1959, pp. 16-37; S.K. De. *Studies in the History of Sanskrit Poetics.* L., 1923, vol. 1; M. Ghosh. *Problems of the Nāṭyaśāstra.*—IHQ, 1930, vol. 6, pp. 71-77; M. Ghosh. *The Nāṭyaśāstra and Bharata Muni.*—IHQ, 1932, vol. 8; P. Kale. *The Theatric Universe (A Study of the Nāṭyaśāstra).* Bombay, 1974; G.I. Miller. *Bharata and Authorship and Age of the Nāṭyaśāstra.*—"Sanskrit Raṅga Annual". Madras, 1971, pp. 189-194; S. C. Mukerjee. The *Nāṭyaśāstra of Bharata.* P., 1926; L. Rocher. *The Textual Tradition of the Bharatyanāṭyaśāstra: A Philological Assessment.* Honolulu, 1974; H.S. Srinivasa. *On the Composition of the Nāṭyaśāstra.* Reinbek, 1980; G.H. Tarleker. *Studies in the Nāṭyaśastra.* Delhi, 1975.

[2] Eclectic in composition, and rather vague in the logic of chapter arrrangement, the treatise has no consistent structure. Though every chapter has a heading, most sections are broader in content than the topic specified in it (this is true to a somewhat lesser extent of chapters on music). Written for the most part in *śloka* verses, it contains over 5,000 couplets. Many chapters also include large prosaic insertions.

[3] Early the *Nāṭyaśāstra* manuscripts are extremely scanty. The extant ones differ from each other with interpolations and errors inevitable in copying. The text exists in several versions from different times. Despite the varying state of preservation—some have gone down to us in fragments—they are all assumed to ascend to one manuscript which gave rise to a tradition. The book is known to have come to the 10th century in two versions—the more extensive, of 12,000 *ślokas*, by *Vṛddha-Bharata* (Elder Bharata), and the concise, half the length. The former is considered the older and more authentic. Prefaces to Grosset's editions of the text contain analyses of these versions and detailed descriptions of the manuscripts: J. Grosset. *Bharatiya-nāṭya-śāstraṁ: Traite de Bharata sur le theatre.* Texte sanskrite. Paris-Lyon, 1898, tome I, pp. IX-XXIII; see also: *Nāṭyaśāstra with Comment. of Abhinavagupta* with a Preface, Appendix and Index by M. Ramakrishna Kavi. Baroda, 1936, vol. 2, pp. VIII-XXII.

[4] On the datings of the *Nāṭyaśāstra* see: Introduction.—*The Nāṭyaśāstra, ascribed to Bharata Muni.* Sanskrit Text, ed. by M. Ghosh. Calcutta, 1967, vol. 1, pp. 49-82. See also: S.K. De. *Studies in the History of Sanskrit Poetic*, vol. 1, p. 26; S. Konow. *Das indische Drama.* Berlin-Leipzig, 1920, S. 2-4.

[5] We think it essential to trace the history of the *Nāṭyaśāstra* studies at least in brief. It opened in 1865, when the American scholar F.-E. Hall, discoverer of the treatise, published several chapters from it. Chapters XVIII-XX, describing the various types of the drama, and XXXIV, which classified scenic parts and the types of dramatis personae, caught his attention, and he published them as a supplement to the *Daśarūpa*, a 10th century treatise on the drama, to present the *Nāṭyaśastra* as continuing it. (See: *The Daśarūpa of Dhanañjaya*, ed. by F.-E. Hall. Calcutta, 1861-1865). In 1874, the German scholar Heymann (W. Heymann. *Über Bharata's Nāṭyaśāstra.* —Nachrichten von der Königl. Gesellschaft der Wissenschaften und der Universitat zu Gottingen, 1874) published a major part of the treatise on the basis of the South Indian manuscript, and a number of his articles on its study problems, which enabled a wide range of researchers

to start extensive studies of the *Nāṭyaśāstra*. The French Sanskritist P. Regnaud, the leading figure among these scholars, prepared a critical edition and translation of Chapter XVII in 1880-1881 (*Le dix-septieme chapitre du Bharatiya-nāṭyaśāstra.* — Annals du Musee Guimet. P., 1880, tome I) and Chapters XV and XVI in 1884 (*Le metrique de Bharata, texte sanskrite de deux chapitres du Nāṭyaśāstra publie pour lapremiere fois et suivi d'une interpretation francaise.*—Annals du Musee Guimet. P., 1884, tome II). Regnaud was mainly interested in sections on the language of the drama and classification principles of Sanskrit- and Prakrit-speaking dramatis personae. Simultaneous analises of these chapters and the language and style of the treatise itself allowed him to draw essential conclusions on the time when the *Nāṭyaśāstra* was written.

In continuation of Regnaud's works, his pupil J. Grosset published a critical edition and translation of Chapter, XXVII in 1888. The musical theory of the *Nāṭyaśāstra* deserved the greatest interest, to his mind. In the late 1880s, he started a complete critical edition of the treatise based on all manuscripts known at the time—a work up to the highest contemporary scientific standards. Volume I appeared in 1898 (*Bharatiya-nāṭya-śāstraṁ: Traite de Bharata sur le theatre. Texte sanscrite.* Paris-Lyon, 1898, tome I). The following never came out.

The Sanskrit text of the *Nāṭyaśāstra* was published in Bombay, 1894, by two Indian scholars, Śivadatta and Parab (*The Nāṭyaśāstra*, ed. by Śivadatta and K.P. Parab.—*Kāvyamālā*. Bombay, 1894, vol. 42). Based on only two manuscripts, the work failed to meet most requirements to a critical edition. It wasn't the authors' goal, for that matter—they meant merely to demonstrate the nature of the ancient Indian drama theory. Another edition came out in Benares, 1929 (*Bharata muni-pranitaṁ Nāṭyaśāstraṁ*—Kashi Sanskrit Series. Benares, 1929), followed by Kedarnath's (*Naṭyaśāstra of Bharata Muni*. Ed. by Kedarnath. Bombay, 1942).

Of major importance for the studies of the treatise was the 1936 Baroda edition of Volume 1, edited by Ramakrishna Kavi and comprising Chapters I to VII with Abhinavagupta's comments. His work put the scholar face to face with many obscure or misrepresented passages in the original. His reconstructions and clarifications proceeded from a large number of manuscripts compared, and the gaps were filled in with the help of Abhinavagupta's comments. Volume 2, with Chapters VIII to XVIII, came out in 1936, and 3 (Chapters XIX-XXVII), 1954. (See: *Nāṭyaśāstra with Comment. of Abhinavagupta* with a Preface, Appendix and Index by M. Ramakrishna Kavi. Baroda, 1926, vol. 1; 1936, vol. 2; 1954, vol. 3). The fourth and last was published by G.S. Pade in 1964, when Ramakrishna Kavi was no more (*Nāṭyaṣāstra with comment. of Abhinavagupta*, ed. by G.S. Pade. Baroda, 1964, vol. 4). At present, this publication is justly considered one of the most comprehensive and profound critical editions of the *Nāṭysaśāstra*. Even this ambitious endeavour, however, failed to solve all interpretation problems due to the poor preservation of extant manuscripts.

M. Ghosh, prominent in the studies of the treatise, prepared a two-volume critical edition of his own, printed in Calcutta (*The Nāṭyaśāstra*, ascribed to Bharata Muni. Sanskrit text, ed. by M. Ghosh. Calcutta, 1967, vol. 1; 1956, vol. 2). It started with the chapters on the music theory comprising Volume 2, published a decade earlier than Volume 1, which contained the rest of the treatise (Chapters I-XXVII). In his reconstruction, based on thorough studies of the manuscripts, Ghosh proceeded from the majority of earlier critical editions. Unable to provide all the variants which he came across in the many extant manuscripts, Ghosh spared no effort to bring his versions into conformity with the other publications, which allowed him to demonstrate as many discrepant versions as possible. He marked what he deemed later interpolations with asterisks. Its many virtues make the Calcutta edition the most convenient for a student of the *Nāṭyaśāstra*. This was why it was used in the present study.

Later decades brought more publications, which we merely enumerate. The Indian scholars Batuka Nath Sharma and Baladev Upadhyay published a one-volume edition in Benares, 1980 (*Nāṭyaśāstraṁ*, ed. by Batuka Nath Sharma and Baladev Upadhyay. Varanasi, 1980). R.S. Nagar put out another, four-volume one in Delhi a year later, complete with Abhinavagupta's comment (*Nāṭyaśāstraṁ with the Abhinavabhārati. Commentary of Abhinavagupta*, ed. by R.S. Nagar. Delhi, 1981, vol. 1-4).

This concise history of the *Nāṭyaśāstra* studies will be incomplete without a mention of its translations into European languages. As far as we know, there are only three unabridged translations, all English. The first, M. Ghosh's—published in 1961, vol. II, and 1967, vol. I—was based on his critical edition (*The Nāṭyaśāstra*, completely translated for the first time from the Original Sanskrit with an Introduction various Notes and Index by Ghosh M. Calcutta, 1967, vol. I; 1961, vol. 2). In his desire to make the text easily comprehensible, the scholar often sacrificed scientific precision. His translation, nevertheless, was of importance for specialists and made the treatise accessible to informed laymen. We can hardly overestimate Ghosh's edition and translation — the cause of a remarkable scholar's lifetime and fundamental contribution into the studies of one of the most interesting and sophisticated ancient Indian treatise.

This remained the only translation for three decades. Two more appeared quite recently. The first, A. Rangacharya's, appeared in Bangalore in 1986 (*Nāṭyaśāstra of Bharata Muni*. English Translation with Critical Notes by Rangacharya A. Bangalore, 1986). Without the chance to see the book, we judge it by its bibliographical description. It came out in one volume, with the translator's critical commentary. The other, 1989, belonged to a team led by Parameśvar Ayer (*The Nāṭya Śāstra of Bharatamuni*. Transl. by a Board of Scholars. Delhi, 1989). Fairly precise, it, however, isn't quite up to the latest standards of ancient manuscript translation. The absence of a reference apparatus, commentaries and variant interpretations are its major drawbacks. It does not even specify the edition from which the translation was made. Only personal acquaintance with the publisher allowed the author of this monograph to learn that it was the Sanskrit text published by Ghosh, whom the team closely followed, especially in the interpretation of special terms, so baffling for translators.

The very fact that the century of the *Nāṭyaśāstra* studies resulted only in three finished translations shows the difficulties which face the students of this treatise. Though written in a comparatively simple Sanskrit, it is hard to understand the text and find an adequate wording for it in other languages. Literary merits come, most often, at the expense of presicion, whereas literal translations are dry-as-dust, over-laconic and barely readable.

[6] Notably, the majority of hypotheses take into consideration both the sacral and the secular origins of the ancient Indian theatre. Only two see it as born outside religion. The first was advanced by R. Pischel at the start of this century (R. Pischel. *Die Heimat des Puppenspiels.—"Hallesche Rektorreden"*. Halle, 1902). This scholar traced the links of the drama with the puppet theatre, which originated, as he thought, in India to spread worldwide. The other belonged to H. Luders,

who traced it to the shadow theatre (H. Luders. *Sitsungsberichte der Königl. Akademie der Wissenschaften* zu Berlin, 1916).

The idea of the religious rite as the root of the drama belonged to M. Müller (M. Müller. *Rig-Veda-Saṁhitā* transl. and expl., 1869, vol. 1) and received support from S. Levi (S. Levi. *Le theatre indien*. P., 1890). Later, this thesis found consistent partisans in Keith (A.B. Keith. *The Sanskrit Drama in its Origin, Development, Theory and Practice*. L., 1924) and Kuiper (F.B.J. Kuiper. *Varuṇa and Vidūśaka. On the Origin of the Sanskrit Drama*. Amsterdam-Oxford-New York, 1979).

Many scholars attempted to reconcile the religious and secular concepts. Hillebrandt (A. Hillebrandt. *Über die Anfange des indischen Dramas*. Munchen, 1914) and after him Konow (S. Konow. *Das indische Drama*) recognized the impact of practical ritualism on the genesis of the drama but thought, nevertheless, that the theatre proper arose from folk spectacles and ritual games. According to Konow, the ancient Indian drama was derived from a synthesis of the ritual pantomime, the shadow theatre and epic recitals (*Ibid*., S. 42-44). Thieme also traced the drama to shadow plays, folk ritual games and the sacral pantomime representing myths and excerpts from epics (P. Thieme, *Das indische Theater*.— H. Kinderman. *Fernőstliches Theater*. Stuttgart, 1966). For reviews of the basic theories of the origin of the ancient Indian drama see: A.B. Keith. *Op.cit*., pp. 15-35, 49-77; L. Renou. *La recherche sur le theatre indien depuis* 1890.—L'annuarie de l'Ecole pratique des hautes etudes, IV section. P., 1963-64, pp. 27-40; P. Thieme. *Op. cit*., S. 26-51; P. Horsch. *Die vedische Gāthā-und-Śloka Literatur*. Bern, 1966, S. 341-343; F.B.J. Kuiper. *Op.cit*., pp. 110-118.

[7] This hypothesis belongs to Müller: M. Müller. *Rig-veda-Saṁhitā*. For discussions of this issue see: S. Levi. *Op.cit*., pp. 301-307; L. Schroeder. *Mysterium und Mimus in Rigveda*. Amsterdam, 1908; S. Konow. *Op.cit*., S.39; P. Horsch. *Op.cit*., S. 329.

[8] A.B.Keith. *Op.cit*., pp. 16-22.

[9] P. Thieme. *Op.cit*., S. 23.

[10] A. Hillebrandt. *Op.cit*., S. 22-24; S. Konow. *Op.cit*., S. 42-44; J. Gonda. *Zur Frage nach dem Ursprung und Wesen des indischen Dramas*.—"Acta Orientalia". 1943, Bd. 19, S. 373-375; A.B. Keith. *Op.cit*., pp. 24-25, 39-40.

[11] F.B.J. Kuiper, *Op.cit*., p. 115; P. Horsch. *Op.cit*., S. 328-329.

[12] For Kuiper's concept, see also: *The Worship of the Jarjara on the Stage*.—IIJ. 1975, vol. XVI, No. 4, pp. 241-268.

[13] F.B.J. Kuiper. *Varuṇa and Vidūśaka*., pp. 113-114.

[14] *Ibidem*, p. 122.

[15] *Ibidem*, p. 115.

[16] *The Vedic Age. The History and Culture of the Indian People*. Ed. R.C. Majumdar. L., 1951, p. 160.

[17] Chapter V of the *Nāṭyaśāstra* characterizes all these parts of the *Pūrvaraṅga* solely from the ritual viewpoint, though the treatise also gives them a detailed musicological treatment (*NŚ*.29.122-156).

[18] As a special part of the *Pūrvaraṅga*, devoted to *Lokapāla* worship, the *Parivartana* shall be distinguished from the *parivartas* repeatedly performed during the ceremony.

[19] Below we substantiate the interpretation of *Śṛṅgāra Rasa* as joyous emotion.

[20] The *Nāṭyaśāstra* devotes as many as six chapters, XXVIII to XXXIII, to the *Gāndharva* music.

[21] Further on, we use the term "dancing steps" for the *Sūcī Cārī* and leave

out their Sanskrit names.

[22] Our interpretation of the *Nāṭyaśāstra* rites proceeds from theoretical ideas of the rite current in contemporary research. For their generalization and basic bibliography on this problem see: V.W. Turner. *Ritual Process. Structure and Antistructure*. Chicago, 1979; F.D.K. Bosch. *The Golden Germ. An Introduction to Indian Symbolism*. The Hague, 1960; Ph.L. Tobing. *The Structure of the Toba-Batak Belief in the High God*. Amsterdam, 1956; F.B.J. Kuiper. *Cosmogony and Conception: A Query. History of Religions*. Chicago, 1970, vol. 10, No. 2; J. Gonda. *Vedic Ritual*. Leiden, 1980; Ch. Sen. *A Dictionary of the Vedic Ritual*. Delhi, 1978; W. Caland, V. Henry. *L'Agniṣṭoma. Description complete de la forme normale du sacrifice de Soma*. P., 1906-1907, tome 1-2; J.C. Heesterman. *The Ancient Indian Royal Consecration*. The Hague, 1957; S. Levi. *La doctrine du sacrifice dans les Brahmanas*. P., 1898; G.U. Thite. *Sacrifice in the Bhāhmaṇa Texts*. Poona, 1975; U.M. Vesci. *Heat and Sacrifice in the Vedas*. Delhi, 1985; J. Woodroffe. *The Great Liberation (Mahānirvāna Tantra)*. Madras, 1985; R.V. Joshi. *Le ritual de la devotion Kṛṣṇaite*. Pondichery, 1959.

[23] The semantics of the *jarjara* as the *arbor mundi* was pointed out by Kuiper as he interpreted scenic rites in the Vedic cosmogonic context: F.B.J. Kuiper. *Varuṇa and Vidūśaka*., pp. 138, 157-162.

[24] Here we refer to the page after the chapter number because the quotation is in prose and has no verse number.

[25] Of extreme importance to us is that aspect of the semantics of the pure and glowing colour which the ritual practices of many religions closely connect with the supreme being the divinity, as manifest in the shining light. The mythological model of the world makes light/darkness the pivotal opposition reflecting the cosmos/chaos contrast. Many ritual and mythological systems described the division of light from darkness as the emergence of cosmos out of the preternatural chaos. According to the Bible, the organized cosmic space is full of light, while darkness is the property of chaos and hell. Zoroastric dualism is based on permanent struggle between creative Light and destructive Darkness. In the Indian tradition, the amorphous state corresponding to chaos was also characterized by the absent "difference between night and day" (ṚV.X.129). In a later Hindu mythologem, the cycle of complete destruction and re-creation of the world corresponded to the idea of Brahmā's "day-and-night".

[26] On the sacral essence of the *Rasa* see: N.R. Lidova. *The Rasa in the System of the Aesthetic Categories of the Nāṭyaśāstra*.—Literature and Culture of Ancient and Medieval India (in print).

[27] See: F.B.J. Kuiper. *Varuṇa and Vidūśaka*., p. 191.

[28] Apart from *Bhāratī Vṛtti*, the *Nāṭyaśāstra* describes three more styles—*Sāttvatī Vṛtti, Arabhatī Vṛtti* and *Kaiśikī Vṛtti* (*NŚ*.22.12-65).

[29] The *Trigata* received a different interpretation in: F.B.J. Kuiper. *Varuṇa and Vidūśaka*., pp. 180-193.

[30] Lambda Scorpii.

[31] *Pāyasa* was a rice cereal boiled in milk with sugar.

[32] *Madhuparka*, or "honey mixture" known even in the Vedic era and used in a number of rites, had five obligatory ingredients—purified melted butter, water, honey, sugar and curd.

[33] Respectively, Aldebaran and Aquila.

[34] *Kṛsarā*, a ritual dish, was made of milk, rice and sesame seed.

[35] Notably, the type and particular kinds of the ritual offerings fully coincided

with those known in the Vedic time and specified in the *Bhāhmaṇas*. Thus, the *Śatapatha Brāhmaṇa* recommends gifts of gold, garments, cows and horses to remunerate priests who perform the *yajña* (*ŚBr*.IV.3.4.7).

[36] *Ārdrā*, Alpha Orioni; *Maghā*, Regulus, of Alpha Leonis; *Yāmyā*, Musca; *Aśleṣā*, Hydra.

[37] Cubit, apporx. 45 centimentres, or 18 inches.

[38] Cf. the Christian rites of church foundation and consecration as described in the missal.

[39] Probably, these were the priestesses who danced in the initial *Parivarta* of the *Pūrvaraṅga*.

[40] See: F.B.J. Kuiper. *Varuṇa* and *Vidūśaka*., pp. 113-114. The author dedicated an article to the same topic: *The Worship of the Jarjara on the Stage*, pp. 241-248.

[41] The *Brāhmaṇas* provide a detailed description of the *Agniṣṭoma*-type rite, e.g., the respective sections of the *Śatapatha Brāhmaṇa*, which characterize the *Somayajña*. Noteworthy of the studies on this topic are: W. Caland, V. Henry. *L'Agniṣṭoma., tome* 1-2; G.M. Thite. *Sacrifice in the Bhāhmaṇa Texts*.

[42] For a description of the *yūpa*, see the *Śatapatha Brāmaṇa* (*ŚBr*.III.6.4.1-8). The *Nāṭyaśāstra* provides the basic characteristics of the *jarjara* in Chapter XXIII, devoted to stage props, costumes and make-up. With reference to the authoritative Viśvakarman, the treatise prescribed to make a *jarjara* of a five-section bamboo stem 4.5 cubits (approx. 2 m) long. The stem preliminarily received rich offerings of flowers and incense, was greased with a mixture of butter and honey, and a *pūjā* was performed in its honour, similar to what was performed in honour of the *jarjara* elevation (*NŚ*.23.171-178).

[43] Though fully aware of how conventional the term "Hinduism" is, with its relatively recent origin, and coming of another tradition, we use it, nevertheless, as a customary word which designates the medieval *Āgamic* culture in scholarly literature.

[44] Cf., for instance, the description of a Kṛṣṇa rite in: R.V. Joshi. *Le rituel de la devotion Kṛṣṇaite*. Pondichery. 1949.

[45] On the *Āgamic* tradition, see: A. Avalon. *Śakti and Śākta*. London-Madras, 1920; Ch. Chakravarty. *The Tantras. Studies on their Religion and Literature*. Calcutta, 1972; J. Gonda. *Medieval Religious Literature in Sanskrit*. Wiesbaden, 1977; T. Goudriaan, S. Gupta. *Hindu Tantric and Śākta Literature*. Wiesbaden, 1981; H.W. Schomerus. Der *Śaiva-Siddhanta*. Liepzig, 1912; J. Schoterman. The *Saṭsāhasva Saṁhitā*. Leiden, 1982; J.G. Woodroffe. *Introduction to Tantra Śāstra*. Madras, 1963; Ph. Rawson. *Tantra*. L., 1973; A. Bharati. *The Tantric Tradition*. L., 1969.

[46] This book uses critical editions of three *Śaiva Āgamas: Ajitāgama*, crit. ed. by N.R. Bhatt. Pondichery, 1964, vol. 1; *Rauravāgama*, crit. ed. by N.R. Bhatt. Pondichery 1961, vol. 1; *Mṛgendrāgama*, crit. ed. by N.R. Bhatt. Pondichery, 1962, vol. 1. Of these, the *Ajita* and *Raurava* belong to the basic *Āgamas*, and the *Mṛgendra* to the supplementary, *Upa-Āgamas*. See also a description of the *Āgamic* initiation rite in: T.A. Gopinatha Rao. *Elements of Hindu Iconography*. Madras, 1916, vol. 2, part I, pp. 11-12.

[47] For general characteristics of the 16 parts of the *Āgamic pūjā* see: A. Avalon. *Śakti and Śākta*., p. 522; B. Walker. *Hindu World. An Encyclopedic Survey of Hinduism*. L., 1968, vol. 2, pp. 606-610.

[48] On the meaning of the *Mudrā* gestures in the *Āgamic* rite see: J. Przyliski. *Mudrā.—Indian Culture*. Calcutta, 1936, vol. 2, No. 4, pp. 715-719.

[49] See also: S.V. Gopinath, Ravana Rao. *The Classical Dance Poses of India.* Madras, 1955.

[50] Hypotheses of this kind are exemplified by the concepts of Ṛgvedic dialogical hymns as sources of the drama. See: M. Müller. Ṛgveda-Saṁhitā, vol. 1; S. Levi. *Le theatre indien*; L. Schoreder. *Mysterium und Mimus in Ṛgveda.* Amsterdam, 1908. Another source of the drama is seen in the Vedic rites of the *Somakrayaṇa* and *Mahāvrata.* See: A. Hillebrandt. *Über die Anfange des indischen Dramas,* S. 22-24; S. Konow. *Das indische Drama,* S. 42-44; J. Gonda. *Zur Frage nach dem Ürsprung und Wesen des indischen Dramas.*—"Acta Orientalia", 1943, Bd. 19, S. 373-375.

[51] No hypothesis is more indicative in this respect than Kuiper's, as he traces the link between the Vedic god Varuṇa, the *Jumbaka,* a participant of the *Aśvamedha* Vedic rite, and the *Vidūśaka,* who became a hero in the Sanskrit drama. See: F.B.J. Kuiper. *Varuṇa and Vidūśaka.*

[52] See: A.B. Keith. *The Sanskrit Drama.,* pp. 36-38.

[53] On the styles see: M.Ch. Byrski. *Methodology of the Analysis of Sanskrit Drama.* Warszawa, 1979, pp. 47-48; V. Raghavan. *The Vrttis.*—"*Journal of Oriental Research*". Madras, 1960, vol. 6, part. 4, pp. 346-370; 1961, vol. 7, part. 1, p. 48; vol. 7, part. 2, pp. 91-112; S. Chattopadhyaya. *Nāṭaka-lakṣaṇa-ratna-kośa. In the Perspective of Ancient Indian Drama and Dramaturgy.* Calcutta, 1974, pp. 217-220.

[54] On the *Samavakāra* see: K.H. Trivedi. Samavakāra.—"*Journal of the Oriental Institute*", University of Baroda, 1965, vol. 15, No. 2, pp. 197-202; E.W. Marasinghe. *The Sanskrit Theatre and Stagecraft.* Delhi, 1989, pp. 441-445.

[55] "While discharging his duty if one attains desired welfare and one adopts means like observing vows, austerity and penance, this is to be known as *Dharma Śṛṅgāra*" (*NŚ*.20.73).

"If through wealth anything desired is obtained by diverse means or if woman's love and enjoyment of pleasure with them is for some material gain, it is an instance of *Artha Śṛṅgāra*" (*NŚ*.20.74).

"Where there is seduction of a maiden or the mutually consented intercourse between a man and a woman giving them excitement and pleasure, it is called *Kāma Śṛṅgāra*" (*NŚ*.20.75).

[56] See: *Ādiparva.*—*Mahābhārata,* transl. into English prose. Calcutta, 1884, vol. 1, pp. 78-83.

[57] *The Saṃghātaka,* lit., Struggle, is meant here.

[58] As we see it, another kind of the *Sāttvatī Vṛtti* is meant here — the *Utthāpaka,* lit., Excitation, which obliges the opponents to show off their power and superiority in some way.

[59] *Ādiparva,* p. 82.

[60] *Ibidem,* p. 83.

[61] *The Saṃkṣiptaka,* lit., Concision, is meant here.

[62] See: J. Dumezil. *Le festin d'immortalite. Etude de mythologie comparee indo-europeenne.* P., 1924.

[63] See: K.F. Geldner. *Festgruss an Rudolf von Roth.* Stuttgart, 1893, S. 192. We did not take into consideration the most disputable concepts, as, for instance, Slater's hypothesis of the Egyptian impact on pre-Āryan Indian culture. In *Amṛta,* he saw an Egyptian palm juice drink imported via Mesopotamia in the Dravidian era and later inherited by the Āryans (G. Slater. *The Dravidian Elements in Indian Culture.* L., 1924, p. 78).

For a comparative analysis of the many versions of the *Amṛtamanthana* myth see: K. Rüping. *Amṛtamanthana und Kūrma-Avatāra. Ein Beitrag zur puranischen Mythen-und Religionsgeschichte.* Wiesbaden, 1970.

[64] *Ādiparva,* p. 80.

[65] Cf. Elizarenkova's translation of *Ṛgveda* (*Maṇḍalas* I-IV. Translated, compiled, preface and annotated by T.Y. Elizarenkova. Moscow, 1989 / in Russian/)

> There where the pestle is tied
> like reins for driving...
>
> (*ṚV*.I.28.4)

See also the translation by R.I.H. Griffith: *The Hymns of the Rigveda.* Translated with a Popular Commentary. Benares, 1986 (2nd ed.)

> There where the woman marks and learns the pestle's constant rise and fall...
>
> (*ṚV*.I.28.3)

[66] Our attention was attracted to this fact by Dr. L.I. Kulikov, to whom we express gratitude for priceless linguistic consultations as we translated the Ṛgveda and other texts from the Sanskrit.

[67] See: W. Norman Brown. *The Creation Myth of the Rig Veda.—"Journal of the American Oriental Society".* 1942, vol. 62, pp. 85-98; F.B.J. Kuiper. *Cosmogony and Conception: A Query.—"History of Religions".* Chicago, 1970, vol. 10, No. 2, pp. 91-138; and *Ancient Indian Cosmogony.* Delhi, 1983.

[68] In some other versions of this myth, *soma* was stolen from the gods by another celestial maiden— for instance, *Gāyatrī*, personification of the Vedic verse metre. Cf.: " Soma was there. The Devas sent Gayatri, saying, 'Bring that Soma.'" Quot. from F.B.J. Kuiper. *An Indian Prometheus?—Asiatische Studien.* Zeitschrift der Schweizerischen Gesellscaft fur Asienkunde. XXXV. Bern, 1971. S. 95. See also: *AitBr*.III.25.I; 26.1-3.

[69] See : E.W. Hopkins. *The Religions of India.* New Delhi, 1970, p. 408; and *Epic Mythology.—Grundriss der Indo-Arischen Philologie.* Strassbourg, 1915, Bd. III, H. 1.

[70] The translation was made with the help of : *The Bṛhadāranyaka Upaniṣad with the Comment. of Śankarācārya,* transl. by Swami Mādhavananda. Calcutta, 1958 (3rd ed.).

[71] See: *Karṇaparva.—Mahābhārata,* transl. into English prose. Calcutta, 1889, vol. 8.

[72] See: R.G. Bhandarkar. *Vaiṣṇavism, Śaivism and Minor Religious Systems,* Varanasi, 1965.

[73] G. Ch. Tripathi. The Legend of the Destruction of Tripura and its Vedic Origin.—*"Amṛtadhara".* Delhi, 1984, pp. 445-455; Bh. S. Mukhopadhyaya. The Tripura Episode in Sanskrit Literature.—*"Journal of Gaṅganatha Jha Research Institute".* 1951, vol. VIII, pp. 371-395.

[74] J. Gonda. *Change and Continuity in Indian Religion.* The Hague, 1965.

[75] See: J.A.B. van Buitenen. *The Pravargya, an Ancient Indian Iconic Ritual.* Poona,1968.

[76] See: C. C. Kashikar. *Apropos of the Pravargya.* —"Centre of Advanced Study in Sanskrit" University of Poona. 1972, Stud. 1, pp. 1-10.

[77] See: H. W. Bailey. Cognates of Pūjā.—"*The Adyar Library Bulletin*", 1961, vol. XXV, part 1-4, p. 2.

[78] See: J. N. Farquhar. Temple and Image Worship in Hinduism.—"*Journal of the Royal Asiatic Society*". 1928, vol. 1, pp. 15-23.

[79] See: P.Thieme. Pūjā.—"*Journal of Oriental Research*". Madras, vol. 27, pp. 1-16. The researcher thinks the root "pūj" genetically linked with the Sanskrti "*pṛc*", changed after the following pattern: *pṛncaṁ—kṛpuncaṁ—kṛ-pūjaṁ.*

[80] See: H.W Bailey. *Op. cit.*, pp. 1-2; R. Radhakrishnan. On Pūjā—"*Indian Linguistic*". 1965-67, vol. 26, pp. 225-228.

[81] See. *The Vedic Age. The History and Culture of the Indian People*, p. 160.

[82] See: J. Charpentier. The Meaning and Etymology of Pūjā.—"*Indian Antiquary*". Bombay, 1927, vol. LVI, pp. 93-98, 130-135.

[83] See: R. Radhakrishnan. *Op. cit.*, p. 225.

[84] See: M. Mayrhofer. *Kurzgefasstes etymologischer Worterbuch des Altindischen*. Heidelberg, 1956, Bd. II.

[85] See: R. N. Dandekar. *Some Aspects of the History of Hinduism*. Poona, 1967, p. 17.

[86] See, in particular, J. Gonda's works generalising on a vast number of books on this subject: *Change and Continutiy. . . Visnuism and Shivaism*. L., 1970; *Aspects of Early Visṇuism*. Delhi, 1969.

[87] See: J. Gonda. *Medieval Religious Literature in Sanskrit*, p. 5.

[88] See: A. A. Macdonell. *A History of Sanskrit Literature*. L., 1905, p. 352.

[89] See, in particular: B. Dagens *Architecture in the Ajitāgama and the Rauravāgama*. New Delhi, 1984.

[90] On the *Guhā* temple see: S. Kramrisch. *Indian temple*. Calcutta, 1946, vol. I p. 171; P.K. Acharya. *A Dictionary of Hindu Architecture*. Allahabad, 1927, p. 270.

[91] According to one hypothesis, the ancient Indian theatre originated from the puppet theatre— hence the term *Sūtradhāra* , which is thus to be interpreted as "he who holds the strings" See: R. Pischel. *Die Heimat des Puppensiels*— "Hallesche Rektorreden". Halle, 1900.

[92] The *Āgamas* also contain references to *Nāṭmandiras* and *Nāṭśālās* used in ritual purpose. See, e.g.: *Suprabhedāgama*, XXXI, 96-98.

[93] See: Gopinatha Rao. *Elements of Hindu Iconography*. N. Y., vol. 1, part 2, app. A.

[94] For details see: P. Brown. *Indian Paintings*. L., 1918; E.B. Havell. *Indian Sculpture and Painting*. L., 1908; Bachhoffer. *Early Indian Sculpture*. 1929, vol. 1-2; S. Kramrisch. *Treatise on Indian Painting and Image Making*. Calcutta, 1928; I.N. Banerjee, Gopinatha Rao. *The development of Hindu Iconography*. Calcutta, 1941.

[95] In fact, fundamentals of the colour theory were formulated in ancient Indian art on the basis of the dancing and theatre make-up. Notably, the very term *vartana*, "modelling", used in the early texts, was also, to all appearances, borrowed from dancing and derived from make-up. In the *Nāṭyaśātra*, the word *vartana*—ascending to the root *vṛt*, "rotate"—means the applying of paint on the rounded surface of the human limbs, i.e., make-up. Transferred to painting, the word received a new meaning—the portrayal of the three-dimensional human body by means of paints. This borrowing of the techniques and terms from dancing perfectly agreed with the general message of the ancient Indian treatise on art *Viṣṇudharmottara*, which repeatedly demanded that painting borrow certain precepts from dancing. Thus, the closing passage of the *Sūtra* on Painting says:

" That which is not mentioned here is to be known from the dancing [craft]. What is not specified in [the rules of] dancing shall not be added unto the rules of painting".

[96] See: note 45.

[97] See: J. Gonda. *Medieval Religious Literature in Sanskrit.*

[98] See: P.V. Kane. *History of Dharmaśāstra.* Poona, 1941, vol. 2, part. 2, pp. 709-730.

[99] See: P. Brown. *Indian Architecture* (Buddhist and Hindu Period). Bombay, 1942.

[100] See: A. Weber. *Akademische Vorlesungen über indische Literaturgeschichte.* Berlin, 1876; S. Konow. *Das indische Drama;* A. Hillebrandt. *Über die Anfange des indischen Drama;* M. Ch. Byrski. *Concept of Ancient Indian Theatre.* New Delhi, 1975.

[101] See, in particular, Kāśika's commentary to *Pāṇ.* IV. 3.129: *"naṭa śabdāpi dharmāmnāyayoreva bhavati"*. On the medieval *Āmnāya* system see: T. Goudriaan, S. Gupta. *Hindi Tantric and Śākta Literature,* p. 17.

[102] See: V.S. Agrawala. *India as Known to Pāṇini.* Lucknow, 1953, pp. 338-339.

[103] J. Gonda. *Medieval Religious,* p. 5.

[104] This is borne out by Pāṇini's commentators, who analysed the rule of the changes in the names of gods whose images serve to earn a living. As they had it, the grammarian meant the lower Brahmin groups, who do not trade in holy images but place them "from door to door". See: *Aṣṭādhyāyī of Pāṇini.* Ed. and transl. into English by S. Vasu. Delhi, 1962, vol. 2, p. 975.

[105] The edicts of Aśoka (3rd century B.C.) provide vital historical testimony to this point in the *Nāṭyaśāstra.* Thus, the Great Rock Edict No. 4 says: " In olden times, deprivation of life and harm done on living being.., derision of the Brahmins and *Śramaṇas* [constantly] grew throughout centuries. Now, thanks to the *Dharma* practice of King Piyadasi, Pleasing to the Gods, the sound of the drums has become the sound of the *Dharma* , and the people have seen spectacles with celestial chariots, elephants, conflagrations and other marvellous spectacles" (Translations made from: *Corpus inscriptionum indicarum.* L., 1925, vol. 1. See also: H. Luders. *Mathura Inscriptions.* B., 1961; *Epigraphia indica.* Delhi, 1902-1903, vol. VII). Like the *Nāṭyaśāstra,* this text describes the preceding centuries as the time of depravity and impiety. Characteristically, the improvement of the moeurs is connected not merely with the dissemination of the new religious ethics (Aśoka' *Dharma*) but—even more important in this context—with the newly accepted practice of spectacles, by which mystery plays with plots borrowed from mythology are, doubtless, meant. Also notable is the coincidence of the generalised features of these spectacles with the descriptions of the plots which the *Nāṭyaśāstra* specifies for the *Samavakāra*—both mention a fire, an elephant, etc. Other edicts of Aśoka also mention spectacles. In particular, Edict No. 8 contains such a passage: "The following is arranged [by Aśoka]: spectacles and spread of the gifts among *Śramaṇas* and Brahmins; spectacles and distribution of gold among the elders; and for rural dwellers, spectacles, instruction in *Dharma* and talks on *Dharma*". Thus, as early as the 3rd century B.C., spectacles were part and parcel of the official religious cult which sought to make peace among the various confessions and unite them. As Aśoka's edicts show, these spectacles were widespread in all social strata. If we assume that they had appeared before Aśoka's reign, we get another oblique proof that theatrical tradition originated about the mid-1st millennium B.C.

BIBLIOGRAPHY

Acharya P. K. A Dictionary of Hindu Architecture. L., 1927.

Agrawala V.S. India as known to Pāṇini. Lucknow, 1953.

Aitareya-Brāhmaṇa. Transl. by Keith A.B. Cambridge, 1920.

Aiyangar J.P. South Indian Customs. Madras, 1925.

Aiyangar K.S. Some Contributions of South India to Indian Culture. Calcutta, 1923.

Aiyyar V.N. Origin and Early History of Shaivism in South India. Madras, 1936.

Ajitāgama. Crit. ed. by Bhat N.R. Pondichery, 1964, vol. 1-2.

Anand M.R. The Indian Theatre. L., 1950.

Apte V.M. Social and Religious Life in the Gṛhya-Sūtras. Ahmedabad, 1939.

The Arts of India. Oxford, 1981.

The Aṣṭādhyāyī. Transl. by Vasu S. Delhi, 1962, vol. I-III.

Auboyer J. L'Ancienneti du Culte des Images. P., 1955.

Avalon A. Principles of Tantra. L., 1916.

Avalon A. Śakti and Śākta. London-Madras, 1920.

Awasthi S. Indian Traditional Theatre.—"Arts of Asia". 1974, vol. 4, No. 2.

Bachhofer L. Early Indian Sculpture. P., 1929, vol. I-II.

Bagchi P. C. Pre-Dravidian and Pre-Aryan in India. Calcutta, 1929.

Bailey H.W. Cognates of Pūjā.—"The Adyar Library Bulletin". 1961, vol. XXV, part 1-4, p. 1-12.

Banerjee J.N. Development of Hindu Iconography. Calcutta, 1956, vol. 1-2.

Banerjee J.N. The Hindu Concept of God.—The Religions of the Hindus. N.Y., 1953.

Barnett L.D. Hindu Gods and Heroes. L., 1922.

Barth A. The Religions of India. L., 1908.

Bernier R.M. Temple Arts of Kerala. New Delhi, 1982.

Bhandarkar R.G. Vaiṣṇavism, Śaivism and Minor Religious Systems. Varanasi, 1965.

Bhat G.K. Sanskrit Drama: Problems and Perspectives. Delhi, 1985.

Bhat G.K. Tragedy and Sanskrit Drama. Bombay, 1974.

Bhat G.K. The Origin of Nāṭya: Role of Śiva.—"Annals of the Bhandarkar Oriental Research Institute". Poona, 1975, vol. LVI.

Bhatt S.C. Drama in Ancient India. New Delhi, 1961.

Bhattacharya B. The Cult of Brahma. Patna, 1957.

Bhattacharya B.C. Indian Images. Calcutta, 1921.

Bhattacharya N.N. Ancient Indian Rituals and Their Social Contents. L., 1975.

Bhattacharya N.N. History of Indian Cosmogonical Ideas. New Delhi, 1971.

Bhattacharya S. The Indian Theogony. Cambridge, 1970.

Bouquet A.C. Hinduism. L., 1948.

Brown P. Indian Paintings. L., 1908.

van Buitenen J.A.B. The Pravargya, an Ancient Indian Iconic Ritual described and annotated. Poona, 1968.

Byrski M.Ch. Can Sanskrit Drama tell us anything more?— "Educational Theatre Journal". 1975, vol. 27, No. 4, pp. 445-452.

Byrski M.Ch. Concept of Ancient Indian Theatre. New Delhi, 1974.

Byrski M.Ch. Methodology of the Analysis of Sanskrit Drama. Warszawa, 1979.

Caland W., Henry V. L'Agniṣṭoma, Description Complete de la forme normale du Sacrifice de Soma. P., 1906, vol. 1; 1907, vol. 2.

Caracchi P. La Presenza Divina Della Murti Secondo i Purana.—"Indologia Taurinensia". Torino, 1978.

Cargill O. Drama and Liturgy. N.Y., 1969.

Chakravarty Ch. The Tantras. Studies on their Religion and Literature. Calcutta, 1972.

Charpentier J. The Meaning and Etimology of Pūjā.— "Indian Antiquary". Bombay, 1927, LVI, pp. 93-98, 130-135.

Chattopadhyaya S. Evolution of Hindu Sects. Delhi, 1970.

Chattopadhyaya S. Nāṭaka-lakṣaṇa-ratna-kośa. In the Perspective of Ancient Drama and Dramaturgy. Calcutta, 1974.

Chaudhuri H.K. Yajña: Its Magical Significance.—"Bhavan's Journal". Bombay, 14 (7).

Coomaraswamy A.K. Hindu Theatre.—IHQ. 1933, vol. IX.

Dagens B. Architecture in the Ajitāgama and the Rauravāgama. New Delhi, 1984.

Dandekar R.N. Some Aspects of the History of Hinduism. Poona, 1967.

Danielou A. Hindu Politheism. L., 1964.

Das D.K. The Yajña: The Sacrifice in Hinduism. Delhi, 1911.

Dasgupta H.N. The Indian Stage. Calcutta, 1934, vol. I; 1938, vol. 2.

Dasgupta S.B. Obscure Religious Cults. Calcutta, 1946.

Datta K. Prologues and Epilogues in Sanskrit Drama.—"Our Heritage". 1957, vol. 5.

Daumal R. Bharata. L'Origine du theatre. P., 1970.

Dave N. Nāndī in Theory.—IHQ. 1941, vol. XVII, pp. 359-369.

De S.K. History of Sanskrit Literature. Calcutta, 1962.

De S.K. The Problem of Bharata and Adī-Bharata.—De S.K. Some Problems of Sanskrit Poetics. Calcutta, 1959.

De S.K. Studies in the History of Sanskrit Poetics. L., 1923, vol. 1.

Devasthali G.V. Religion and Mythology of the Brāhmaṇas. Poona, 1965.

Dowson J. A Classical Dictionary of Hindu Mythology and Religion. L., 1957.

Dubois S.A. Hindu Manners, Customs and Ceremonies. Oxford, 1953.

Dumesil G. Le Festin d'immortalite. Etude de Mythologie Comparee Indo-Europienne. P., 1924.

Dumont P. E. L'Agnihotra. Baltimore, 1939.

Dumont P. E. L'Aśvamedha. Paris-Louvain, 1927.

Elmore W.T. Dravidian Gods in Modern Hinduism. Madras, 1925.

Farquhar J.N. The Crown of Hinduism. Oxford, 1913.

Farquhar J.N. Temple and Image Worship in Hinduism.—JRAS. L., 1928, pp. 15-23.

O'Flaherty W.D. Asceticism and Eroticism in the Mythology of Śiva. L., 1973.

Frankfort H. The Art and Architecture of the Ancient Orient. Harmondsworth, 1954.

Gaster T.H. Thespis. Ritual, Myth and Drama in the Ancient Near East. N.Y., 1950.

Ghosh M.A. Aśvaghoṣa and the Nāṭyaśāstra.—IHQ. 1951, vol. XXVII.

Ghosh M.A. Contributions to the History of the Hindu Drama. Its Origin, Development and Diffusion. Calcutta, 1957.

Ghosh M.A. Hindu Theatre.—IHQ. 1933, vol. IX.

Ghosh M.A. The Nāṭyaśāstra and Bharatamuni.—IHQ. 1932, vol. VIII.

Ghosh M.A. Problems of the Nāṭyaśāstra.—IHQ. 1930, vol. VI, pp. 71-77.

Ghosh P. Ch. Origin of the Durga Pūjā. Calcutta, 1874.

Gonda J. Ancient Indian Kingship from the Religious Point of View.—"Numen". Leiden, 1956-57, No. 3-4.

Gonda J. Aspects of Early Viṣṇuism. Delhi, 1969.

Gonda J. Change and Continuity in Indian Religion. The Hague, 1965.

Gonda J. The Indra Festival According to the Atharvavedins.—"Journal of American Oriental Society". 1967, No.87, pp. 413-429.

Gonda J. Les Religious de L'Inde. P., 1963, vol. 1; 1965, vol. 2.

Gonda J. Medieval Religious Literature in Sanskrit. Wiesbaden, 1977.

Gonda J. Notes on Brahman. Utrecht, 1950.

Gonda J. The Ritual Sūtras. Wiesbaden, 1977.

Gonda J. The Savayajñas. Amsterdam, 1965.

Gonda J. Veda und Alterer Hinduismus. Stuttgart, 1960.

Gonda J. Viṣṇuism and Śivaism: A Comparison. L., 1970.

Gonda J. Zur Frage nach dem Ursprung and Wesen des indischen Dramas.—"Acta Orientalia". 1943, vol. 19, S.B29-428.

Gopal Ram. India of Vedic Kalpasūtras. Delhi, 1959.

Gopinath S.V., Ravana Rao. The Classical Dance Poses of India. Madras, 1955.

Gopinatha Rao. Elements of Hindu Iconography. Madras, 1916, vol. 1, part 1-2; vol. 2, part 1-2 (repr.: Delhi, 1985).

Gordon D.H. The Pre-Historic Background of Indian Culture. Bombay, 1958.

Goudriaan T., Gupta S. Ḥindu Tantric And Śākta Literature. Weisbaden, 1981.

Gupta C.B. Indian Theatre—Past and Present. Benares, 1954.

Haas C.O. Translation of the Daśarūpa by Dhanaṭjaya. N.Y., 1962.

Hariappa H.L. Rigvedic Legends Through the Ages. Poona, 1953.

Havell E.B. The Ancient and Medieval Architecture of India. New Delhi, 1972.

Hazra R.C. Studies in the Puranic Records on Hindu Rites and Customs. Dacca, 1940.

Heesterman J.C. The Ancient Indian Royal Consecration. The Hague, 1957.

Held G.J. The Mahābhārata, an Ethnological Study. London-Amsterdam, 1935.

Hillebrandt A. Ritual-Literatur. Vedische Opfer und Zauber. Strassburg, 1897.

Hillebrandt A. Uber die Anfange des indischen Dramas. Munchen, 1914.

Hiltebeitel A. The Ritual of Battle. Ithaca-London, 1976.

Hopkins E.W. Epic Mythology. Strassburg, 1915 (repr.: Delhi, 1974).

Hopkins E.W. The Religions of India. New Delhi, 1970.

Horrwitz E.P. The Indian Theatre. L., 1912.

Horsch P. Die Vedische Gāthā-und-Śloka-Literatur. Bern, 1966.

Hubert H., Mauss M. Sacrifice: Its Nature and Function. University of Chicago Press, 1964.

Hunningher B. The Origin of the Theatre. N.Y., 1961.

Jagirdar R.V. Drama in Sanskrit Literature. Bombay, 1947.

Jaiswal S. Origin of Image Worship and Its Rituals.—"Proceedings of the Indian History Congress, 28th Session". 1966, pp. 58-64.

Jha Sh. Drama—Its Meaning and Purpose. Allahabad, 1929.

Jons V. Indian Mythology. L., 1968.

Joshi R.V. Le Rituel de la Devotion Kṛṣṇaite. Pondichery, 1959.

Kale P. The Theatric Universe (A Study of the Nāṭyaśāstra). Bombay, 1974.

Kane P. V. History of Dharmaśāstra. Ancient and Medieval Religious and Civil Law. Poona, 1930-1962, vol. 1-5.

Kane P. V. History of Sanskrit Poetics. Delhi, 1961.

Kashikar C.C. Apropos of the Pravargya.—"Centre of Advanced Study in Sanskrit". University of Poona. 1972, Stud.1, pp. 1-10.

Keith A.B. A History of Sanskrit Literature. L., 1928.

Keith A.B. The Religion and Philosophy of the Veda and Upanishads. Cambridge, 1925, vol. 1-2.

Keith A.B. The Sanskrit Drama in its Origin, Development, Theory and Practice. L., 1954.

Konow S. Das Indische Drama. Berlin-Leipzig, 1920.

Kramrisch S. The Hindu Temple. Calcutta, 1946, vol. 1-2.

Kramrisch S. Indian Sculpture. L., 1933.

Kramrisch S. The Presence of Shiva. Princeton, 1981.

Kramrisch S. Treatise on Indian Painting and Image Making. Calcutta, 1928.

Kuiper F.B.J. Varuṇa and Vidūśaka. On the Origin of the Sanskrit Drama. Amsterdam-Oxford-New York, 1979.

Kuiper F.B.J. The Worship of the Jarjara on the Stage.—IIJ. 1975, vol. XVI, No.4, pp. 241-268.

Kumarappa Bh. The Hindu Conception of the Deity. L., 1934.

Levi S. Le doctrine du sacrifice dans les Brāhmaṇas. P., 1898.

Levi S. Le theatre indien. P., 1890, vol. 1-2.

Lidova N.R. Ritual Sources of Sanskrit Drama.—Indian Traditions through the Ages. New Delhi, 1990.

Lidova N.R. Raṅgadevatāpūjana in the Nāṭyaśāstra and the Āgamic Rituals.—VIII World Sanskrit Conference. Abstracts. Vienna, 1990.

Luders H. Sitzungsberichte der Konigl. Academic der Wissenschaften. Berlin, 1916.

Macdonell A.A. A History of Sanskrit Literature. L., 1905.

Macdonell A.A. Vedic Mythology. Strassburg, 1897.

Macdonell A.A., Keith A.B. Vedic Index of Names and Subjects. Varanasi, 1958, vol. 1-2.

Mahābhārata. Transl. into English Prose. Calcutta, 1884, vol. 1; 1889, vol. 8.

Majumdar R.C. Ancient India. Varanasi, 1952.

Mankad D.R. Hindu Theatre.—IHQ. 1932, vol. VIII; 1933, vol. IX.

Mankad D.R. The Types of Sanskrit Drama. Karachi, 1936.

Marasinghe E.W. The Sanskrit Theatre and Stagecraft. Delhi, 1989.

Marshall J. Mohenjo-Daro and the Indus Civilisation. L., 1931, vol. III.

Miller G.J. Bharata and the Authorship and Age of the Nāṭyaśāstra.—"Sanskrit Raṅga Annual", Raghavan Felicitation Volume. Madras, 1972, pp. 189-194.

Monier-Williams M. Brahmanism and Hinduism. L., 1891.

Mṛgendrāgama, ed. Bhatt N.R. Pondichery, 1962, vol. 1.

Mukerjee S.C. The Nāṭyaśāstra of Bharata. P., 1926.

Mukhopadhyaya Bh.S. The Tripura Episode in Sanskrit Literature.—"Journal of Gaṅganatha Jha Research Institute". 1951, vol. VIII.

Muūrtipūjā. Bombay, 1902.

Mythes et Legendes Extraits des Brāhmaṇa. P., 1967.

The Nāṭyaśāstra, ed. by Sivadatta and Parab K.P. —"Kāvyamala". Bombay, 1894, vol. 42.

Nāṭyaśāstra of Bharata Muni, ed. by Kedarnath. Bombay, 1942.

Nāṭyaśāstra with Comment. of Abhinavagupta with a Preface, App. and Index by M. Ramakrishna Kavi. Baroda, 1926, vol. 1; 1936, vol. 2; 1954, vol. 3.

Nāṭyaśāstra with Comment. of Abhinavagupta, ed. by Pade J.S. Baroda, 1964, vol. 4.

The Nāṭyaśāstra, ascribed to Bharata Muni. Sanskrit Text, ed. by Ghosh M. Calcutta, 1956, vol. 2; 1967, vol. 1.

Nāṭyaśāstra, ed. by Batuka Nath Sharma and Baladev Upadhyay. Varanasi, 1980.

Nāṭyaśāstra with the Abhinavabhāratī Comment. of Abhinavagupta, ed. by Nagar R.S. Delhi, 1981, vol. 1-4.

The Nāṭyaśāstra. Completely transl. for the first time from the Original Sanskrit with an Introd., Various Notes and Index by Ghosh M. Calcutta, 1961, vol. 2; 1967, vol. 1.

Nāṭyaśāstra of Bharata Muni. English Transl. with Critical Notes by Rangacharya A. Bangalore, 1986.

The Nāṭya Śāstra of Bharatamuni. Transl. by a Board of Scholars. Delhi, 1989.

Notes on the Restoration of a Temple Theatre for the Sanskrit Drama.—"National Centre for the Performing Arts Journal". 1975, vol. IV, No.1, pp. 25-31.

Oldenberg H. Die Religion des Veda. Stuttgart-Berlin, 1923.

Parikh J.T. The Orthodox Tradition about the Origin of Sanskrit Drama.—"Journal of Oriental Institute". University of Baroda, vol. 1, No.4.

Parrinder G. Worship in the World's Religion. L., 1961.

Patañjali. Mahābhāṣya. Bombay, 1932-37, vol. 1-3.

Pathak V.S. History of the Shaiva Cult in Northen India. Varanasi, 1960.

Phillips N. The Evolution of Hinduism. Madras, 1903.

Pischel R. Die Heimat des Puppenspiels.—Hallesche Rectorreden. Halle, 1900.

Potdar K.R. Sacrifice in the Rigveda. Bombay, 1953.

Przyliski J. Mudrā.—"Indian Culture". Calcutta, 1936, vol. 2, No 4, pp. 715-719.

Puri B.N. India in the Time of Patañjali. Bombay, 1958.

Radhakrishnan R. On Pūjā.—"Indian Linguistic". 1965-67, vol. 26, pp. 225-228.

Raghavan V. Ancient Indian Theatre Architecture.—"Journal Triveni". Madras, 1931.

Raghavan V. Hindu Theatre.—IHQ. 1933, vol. IX.

Raghavan V. Sanskrit Drama and Performance.—"The Madras University Journal". 1957, vol. XXIX, No.1.

Raghavan V. The Vṛttis.—JOR. Madras, 1960, vol. 6, part 4, pp. 346-370; 1961, vol. 7, part 1, pp. 33-52; part 2, pp. 91-112.

Rangacharya A. Drama in Sanskrit Literature. Bombay, 1967.

Rauravāgama, ed. Bhatt N.R. Pondichery, 1961, vol. 1.

Ray N. Idea and Image in Indian Art. Calcutta, 1973.

Renou L. Hinduism. N.Y., 1963.

Renou L. Religions of Ancient India. L., 1953.

Renou L. Vocabulaire du rituel vedique. P., 1954.

Rocher L. The Textual Tradition of the Bhāratīyanāṭyaśāstra: A Philological Assessment. Honolulu, 1974.

Rowland B. The Art and Architecture of India. Suffolk, 1959.

Rüping K. Amṛtamanthana und Kūrma-Avatāra. Ein Beitrag zur puranischen Mythen- und Religionsgeschichte. Wiesbaden, 1970.

Sampurnanand. Evolution of the Hindu Pantheon. Bombay, 1963.

Sarma D.S. Hinduism through the Ages. Bombay, 1956.

Sastri H.K. South Indian Images of God and Goddesses. Madras, 1916.

Sastrin H. The Origin of Indian Drama.—"Journal and Proceedings of the Asiatic Society of Bengal". 1909, vol. 5, pp. 351-358.

The Śatapatha-Brāhmaṇa, Transl. by Eggeling J. Delhi, 1978, vol. 1-5.

Scheuer J. Śiva dans le Mahābhārata. P., 1982.

Schroeder L. Mysterium und Mimus im Rigveda. L., 1908.

Shastri S.N. Laws and Practices of Sanskrit Drama. Varanasi, 1961, vol. 1.

Sivaramamurti C. Indian Sculpture. New Delhi, 1961.

Sivaramamurti C. Naṭarāja in Art, Thought and Literature. New Delhi, 1974.

Slater G. The Dravidian Elements in Indian Culture. L., 1924.

Srinivasa A.S. On the Composition of the Nāṭyaśāstra. Reinbek, 1980.

Srinivasan P. R. Inscriptional Evidence on Early Hindu Temples.—"The Adyar Library Bulletin". 1961, vol. XXV, part 1-4, pp. 511-523; vol. XXVI, part 1-2, pp. 1-25.

Tarlekar J.H. Studies in the Nāṭyaśāstra. Delhi, 1975.

Thieme P. Das indische Theater.—Fernostliches Theater. Stuttgart, 1966, pp. 26-51.

Theime P. Pūjā.—JOR. Madras, No.27, pp. 1-16.

Thite G.M. Sacrifice in the Brāhmaṇa-Text. Poona, 1975.

Thite G.M. Vidūśaka: His Ritualistic Background.—"Journal of the University of Poona". 1978, No.43, pp. 9-12.

Tripathi C.Ch. The Legend of the Destruction of Tripura and its Vedic Origin.—Amṛtadhara. Delhi, 1984.

Trivedi K.H. Samavakāra.—"Journal of the Oriental Institute". University of Baroda. 1965, No.2, pp. 197-202.

Tucci G. The Theory and Practice of the Maṇḍala. L., 1961.

Turner V.W. Ritual Process. Structure and Antistructure. Chicago, 1979.

Varadpande M.L. Religion and the Theatre. New Delhi, 1983.

Varma K.M. Nāṭya, Nṛtta and Nṛtya. Bombay, 1957.

Varma L., *Ravi* A. Rituals of Worship. —"The Cultural Heritage of Indian Religions". Calcutta, 1956, vol. 4.

Vatsyayan K. Indian Classical Dance. Calcutta, 1974.

Vatsyayan K. The Square and the Circle of the Indian Art. New Delhi, 1983.

Vatsyayanan K. Traditional Indian Theatre: Multiple Streams. New Delhi, 1980.

The Vedic Age. The History and Culture of the Indian People, ed. Majumdar R.C. L., 1951.

Vidyabhushan A.C. The Origin of Indian Drama.—The Theatre of the Hindus. Calcutta, 1955, pp. 206-216.

The Viṣṇudharmottara. Canon of Proportions, transl. by Kramrisch S. Calcutta, 1928, part I-III.

Vogel J.P. The Woman and Tree or Śālabhaṭjikā in Indian Literature and Art.—"Acta Orientalia". 1929, vol. VII.

Walker B. Hindu World: An Encyclopedic Survey of Hinduism. L., 1968, vol. 1-2.

Weber A. Akademische Vorlesungen uber indische Literatur geschichte. Berlin, 1876.

Wijesekera O.H. Buddhist Evidence for the Early Existance of Drama.—IHQ. 1951, vol. XXVII.

Wilkins W.J. Hindu Mythology Vedic and Pūraṇic L., 1882.

Winternitz M. History of Indian Literature. Calcutta, 1959, vol. 1-3 (repr.: Delhi, 1983).

Woodroff J.G. Introduction to Tantra Śāstra. Madras, 1963.

Woodroff J.G. Tantrik Texts. Madras, 1929.

Woodroff J.G. The World as Power. Madras, 1957.

Yajnik R.K. The Indian Theatre. L., 1933.

Young K. The Drama of the Medieval Church. Oxford, 1933, vol. 1-2.

Zimmer H. The Art of Indian Asia. N.Y., 1955.

Zimmer H. Myths and Symbols in Indian Art and Civilization. N.Y., 1947.

ABBREVIATIONS

IHQ—Indian Historical Quarterly

JRAS—Journal of the Royal Asiatic Society

JOR—Journal of Oriental Research

IIJ—Indo-Iranian Journal

INDEX